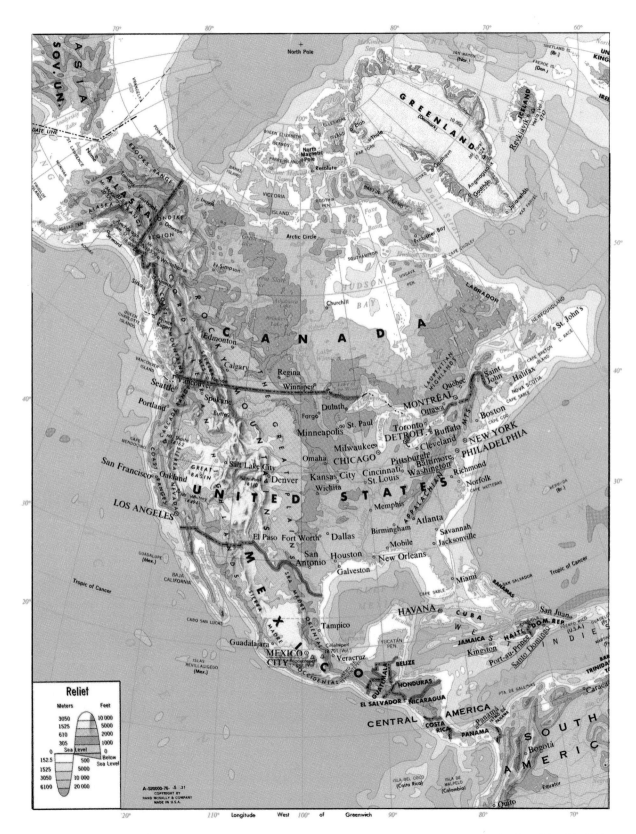

Enchantment of the World

PANAMA

By Ana María B. Vázquez

Consultant: George I. Blanksten, Ph.D., Professor of Political Science, Northwestern University, Evanston, Illinois

Consultant for Reading: Robert L. Hillerich, Ph.D., Visiting Professor, University of South Florida; Consultant, Pinellas County Schools, Florida

CHILDRENS PRESS®
CHICAGO

New high rises in Panama City

Library of Congress Cataloging-in-Publication Data

Vásquez, Ana María B. (Ana María Brull)
  Panama / by Ana María Vásquez.
    p.   cm. – (Enchantment of the world)
  Includes index.
  Summary: Discusses the geography, history, economics,
and culture of Panama.
  ISBN 0-516-02604-6
  1. Panama – Juvenile literature.   [1. Panama.]
I. Title. II. Series.
F1563.2.V39   1991   91-12667
972.87 – dc20   CIP
                                                           AC

Picture Acknowledgments
AP/Wide World Photos: 26 (right), 87 (left), 91 (bottom
left), 93 (left)
The Bettmann Archive: 72 (inset), 80 (left), 82, 87 (inset),
90 (top center and top left), 93 (right)
H. Armstrong Roberts: © **M. Thonig,** 19 (right); © **E.R.
Degginger,** 21 (top right); © **K. Scholz,** 92 (right)
Historical Pictures Service, Chicago: 74, 77, 91 (top left)
Impact Visuals: © **Wim Van Cappellen,** 41; © **Donna
DeCesare,** 42, 43, 44, 53 (right); © **Les Stone,** 105
North Wind Picture Archives: 80 (right), 81 (2 photos), 90
(bottom left)
Odyssey/Frerck/Chicago: 90 (right), 91 (center and right),
95; © **Robert Frerck,** 4, 5, 58 (right), 59 (left), 61 (right), 63
(2 photos), 68 (left), 71 (right), 72, 94, 110, 111 (left);

© **Charles Seaborn,** 22 (bottom right)
Chip and Rosa Maria de la Cueva Peterson: 17 (left)
Photri: 25, 96 (right), 113 (right), 56 (right); © **Leonard Lee
Rue III,** 19 (left)
© **Porterfield/Chickering:** 27 (left), 29 (left)
Reuters/Bettmann Newsphotos: 107
Root Resources: © **Grace H. Lanctot,** 9, 33 (2 photos);
© **Mary Ann Hemphill,** 12; © **Irene E. Hubbell,** 14 (left),
32 (right); © **Connie Bickman,** 17 (right), 51 (left), 64, 68
(right); © **Sally Wiener Grotta,** 84 (top); © **Vera Bradshaw,**
51 (right), 67
© **Bob and Ira Spring:** Cover (inset), 10, 13, 14 (right), 15,
21 (bottom right), 22 (left), 27 (right), 30, 32 (bottom left),
37 (right), 38 (right), 49, 50, 52, 53 (left), 58 (left), 59
(right), 69, 71 (left), 111 (right), 113 (left), 116
Tom Stack & Associates: © **Kevin Schafer,** 20 (top left and
bottom right); © **Jack Swenson,** 20 (top right); © **Wendy
Shattil/Bob Rozinski,** 20 (bottom left); © **Bryon Augustin,**
56 (left)
SuperStock International, Inc.: 24, 55, 65, 115; © **Hubertus
Kanus,** Cover, 6, 96 (left); © **Anthony Mercieca,** 21 (left);
© **Jamie Martorano,** 26 (left); © **John Spooner,** 29 (right);
© **Carole Salman,** 37 (left), 39 (2 photos); © **Eric Carle,** 92
(left); © **Frank T. Wood,** 46; © **Augusts Upitis,** 56 (top), 61
(left), 70
TSW-CLICK/Chicago: © **Tom & Michelle Grimm,** 32 (top
left); © **Danny Lehman,** 38 (left)
UPI/Bettmann Newsphotos: 84 (bottom), 99 (2 photos),
101, 102, 108
Valan: © **Kennon Cooke,** 19 (center); © **Jeff Foott,** 22 (top
right)
Len W. Meents: Maps on 56, 60, 96
**Courtesy Flag Research Center, Winchester,
Massachusetts 01890:** Flag on back cover
Cover: Miraflores Locks, Panama Canal;
        Inset: Cuna Indian girls

Cuna Indians from the San Blas Islands

TABLE OF CONTENTS

The Gaillard Cut (an artificial channel) is where some of
the deepest excavations for the Panama Canal were made.

Chapter 1

CROSSROADS OF
THE WORLD

Some countries are destined to play an important role in the history of the world. Their geography, their natural resources, and their culture can bring to other nations something needed and useful. Such is the case of Panama. Panama is a very small, but important, country. It has occupied a principal place in the commercial history of the world since the sixteenth century and especially since the first quarter of the twentieth century.

If anyone is asked to identify Panama, the first word that usually will come to mind is the canal. This "wonder of the world," an extraordinary feat of engineering most strategically located, changed the navigation patterns of the world. The canal also has given to the country in which it is located the names "Crossroads of the World," "Heart of the Universe," and "Bridge of the Americas." Perhaps the statesmen who forged the independence of this small nation guessed the benefits that would accrue to so many people once the canal was built. When they selected the national motto for their new country, the motto found on their coat of arms, they chose *Pro Mundi Beneficio*, "For the Benefit of the World."

Panama was discovered by a Spanish explorer, Rodrigo de Bastidas, three years after Christopher Columbus first arrived in the New World. It was the first part of the mainland—*Tierra Firme* as the Spaniards called it—to be colonized. Up to then, only some islands in the Antilles archipelago had been discovered, and colonization there had barely begun. It was in Panama that the Pacific Ocean was first seen and explored by Vasco Núñez de Balboa, a discovery that revolutionized Europe. It opened up new vistas both for gold seekers and adventurers in general, as well as for men of science. The limited knowledge of the shape and dimensions of the earth was forever changed. For missionaries, this discovery presented new challenges in the expansion of their God-given mission. After the discovery and conquest of the rich country of Peru, the Isthmus of Panama became the crossroads between the Pacific and the Atlantic coasts.

Because it was very difficult to cross the Andes of South America, riches were brought north from Peru on the Pacific side, across the isthmus to the Atlantic, and then to Europe. Throughout the centuries, people from all over the world chose the Isthmus of Panama as the way to cross from one sea to the other. Before the canal was built, crossing the isthmus was done partly by canoe on the Chagres River and partly on foot or by mule through the dense Darién jungle. This was known as the Cruces Trail.

Panama, a true melting pot of races and cultures, has a most varied population. First there are the native Indians, descendants of the original people who were here when the Spaniards arrived. Then there are descendants of the *conquistadors*, "conquerors," and other Spaniards who kept coming through the centuries; Africans who were brought in as slaves; and Chinese who came to build

Panama City is a lively, sophisticated town.

the railroad. Other settlers were a Scottish group who came to establish a colony in the latter part of the seventeenth century and black islanders from different parts of the West Indies who came looking for work. The French initially came to build a canal, and the Americans who followed them built the definitive canal. In the twentieth century refugees from Central Europe who were fleeing from Nazism, and those who came later escaping from behind the Iron Curtain or from dictatorial regimes in countries such as Cuba, Argentina, and Chile settled in Panama.

All of these and more, people from every part of the world, have come to this Heart of the Universe. Its capital, Panama City, is indeed a bustling cosmopolitan city, a sophisticated mecca of tourism, known the world over for its fascinating past and present.

In the highlands, the village of Boquete has a cool climate and rich soil in which vegetables, fruits, and flowers are grown.

Chapter 2

GEOGRAPHY

The Republic of Panama is located in the isthmus of the same name. Panama is a curved ribbon of land that lies east and west. It is the narrowest section of the Americas between the Atlantic (Caribbean) and the Pacific oceans. It links Central and South America. It is bounded by Costa Rica to the west, Colombia to the east, the Atlantic on the north, and the Pacific on the south.

Panama has an extension of about 400 miles (644 kilometers) from the Costa Rican border to the Colombian border. The shortest distance across the isthmus is about 50 miles (80 kilometers) and the longest is 130 miles (209 kilometers). Panama has an area of 29,762 square miles (77,082 square kilometers). The mainland consists of 29,208 square miles (75,649 square kilometers) and 575 square miles (1,489 square kilometers) are divided among the islands. Panama is about the same size as the state of South Carolina or the European country of Austria.

The borders of Panama have been the cause of many controversies and struggles, particularly the Panama-Costa Rica border. After 116 years of constant friction, the matter was settled in 1941 through the Arias-Calderón Treaty. The Victoria-Vélez 1924 Treaty between Panama and Colombia settled that issue too.

Dense vegetation, such as this rain forest, grows in the lowlands.

THREE DISTINCT AREAS

The Panamanian landscape consists of three distinct areas. The lowlands are hot and comprise 87 percent of the territory. At an altitude of between 2,300 and 4,900 feet (701 and 1,494 meters), the temperate lands comprise 10 percent of the territory. The highlands, or cold lands (not really cold, just cooler), have an altitude of more than 4,900 feet (9,494 meters) and represent only 3 percent of the whole territory.

The Tabasará Mountains extend into Panama from Costa Rica. The highland's highest peak is an extinct volcano, Volcán Barú, in Chiriquí Province. It is 11,401 feet (3,475 meters) high. Other high

A mountain farm village near Volcán Barú in Chiriquí Province

peaks are Cerro Fábrega and Cerro Santiago. The lowlands comprise plains and savannalike areas and jungles. Seventy percent of Panama's territory is jungle. The *Tapón de Darién*, "The Darién Gap," is a jungle area located between Panama and Colombia. The jungle is so dense in vegetation that it is only now being penetrated. In Panama's jungle territory the United States has the Caribbean Jungle Warfare Training Center. There soldiers learn to cope and survive in combat in jungle conditions. This center is scheduled to be removed by the year 2000.

In the mountainous areas in the western provinces, there are resorts where people can enjoy the cooler climate. Some of these are Santa Fe, Bajo Boquete, El Volcán, El Bambito, and Cerro Punta, all in an area called "Little Switzerland."

The Tuira River (left) is in the east near the Colombian border. Fort San Lorenzo (right) was built by the Spaniards to guard the entrance to the Chagres River.

RIVERS AND SEACOASTS

Panama has many rivers, though not large ones. There are approximately five hundred rivers, of which about one-third flow into the Atlantic and about two-thirds into the Pacific. Because the continental divide runs through the isthmus parallel to the coastline, the rivers run from each side of it to the sea. Many rivers are used for transportation or for hydraulic power. The Bayano River has a dam and modern hydraulic installations. It is thanks to the Chagres River and its large amount of water that the Panama Canal could be built. The Chucunague is one of the most tortuous rivers in the world with about two hundred bends. The Sixaola and the Tuira also are important rivers.

Taboga Island, near Panama City, is a popular resort area.

Panama has no natural lakes. The only lake is Gatún Lake, which is man-made, formed by the building of the canal. It is part of the canal route.

Ocean tides in Panama are surprising. They are not the same in the Atlantic and the Pacific. They rise and fall at totally different times and at different intervals.

Panama is a country with a disproportionately huge amount of coastline. The Pacific seaboard is 746 miles (1,201 kilometers) long and the Atlantic seaboard extends for 397 miles (639 kilometers). There are many natural ports, but few have adequate docking facilities. The best ports are Cristóbal on the Atlantic side and Balboa on the Pacific. Puerto Armuelles, Almirante, and Vacamonte are busy ports also. Panama City's port facilities are mainly for small boats used for coastal trade.

POPULATION

For its size, Panama is not a very populous country. It has over 2.6 million inhabitants, of which about 45 percent reside in and near the capital, Panama City. The greater part of Panama's population is *mestizo*, people of mixed background—Hispanic, Indian, and African.

THE CLIMATE

The climate of Panama is tropical and there is little change in temperature year round. The humidity is high and the average temperature ranges from 75 degrees to 88 degrees Fahrenheit (23.8 degrees to 31.1 degrees Celsius), with the temperatures a little cooler in the evening. It also is cooler in the elevated, mountainous regions than it is along the coast.

From April to December there are frequent storms and abundant rainfall. This part of the year, called winter, is the rainy season. During this season there is some rainfall every day, but only for part of the day as the sun shines, at some point, almost every day. This rainfall is vital for the proper functioning of the canal. A drought could create a situation where there would not be enough water for the ships to transit. The dry season, also known as summer, occurs from January to April. During this period, the tradewinds blow and prevent masses of air from clashing.

PLANTS AND ANIMALS

In Panama there is an extraordinary site where study of the flora and fauna takes place. This is the Natural Monument of

Some of the research buildings on Barro Colorado can be seen through the trees (left). A researcher (right) studies a plant.

Barro Colorado, established in 1924, and now under the direction of the Smithsonian Institution of the United States. At the time when the canal was built, the waters of the Chagres River were dammed and a man-made lake called Gatún was created. An island with an elevation of 561 feet (171 meters) above sea level emerged. It is *Barro Colorado*, which means red mud.

Scientists saw the possibility of keeping this island free from extraneous influences, thus creating a virgin reservation where the tropical flora and fauna would be kept unharmed. The island was declared a biological reservation of humid tropical forest—the first one of its kind—and a scientific lab was built. Since then, thousands of scientists (about two hundred every year) have spent time in Barro Colorado, studying the ecology, the evolution, and the behavior of Panama's flora and fauna. On Barro Colorado Island there are over 300 species of timber plants. In the forest one might find 175 tall trees representing 75 different species. There are many other plants—not trees—and new ones are being found constantly. Lianas (climbing plants) are also found here, as in all tropical forests.

There is a richness of fauna also. There are 56 species of bats, as well as tapirs; ñeques, a type of rabbit; sloths; boars; and other animals. Over 350 species of fowl have been reported. Reptiles also are abundant. There are 30 kinds of frogs, 22 species of lizards, and 40 types of snakes. Small insects at Barro Colorado are not overlooked. More than 200 species of ants have been reported, 14 of them known as warrior ants. At least 1,000 different types of grasshoppers are present, along with wild bedbugs, termites, and flying cockroaches. Monkeys of different species wander around the island, which is indeed a zoologist's or botanist's paradise.

When United States President Jimmy Carter negotiated treaties concerning the canal with President Omar Torrijos of Panama in 1977, the importance of the island of Barro Colorado was made evident and a collateral agreement, not related to the canal itself but to Barro Colorado and the land that surrounds it, also was signed. Thus, this area was designated as protected territory. It encompasses several peninsulas in Lake Gatún surrounding the island and it is called the Natural Monument of Barro Colorado.

Of course, the rest of Panama, besides Barro Colorado, is a land of many plants and flowers. The best-known and best-loved flower in Panama is the *Flor del Espíritu Santo*, "Flower of the Holy Spirit," a white, perfumed orchid that looks like a dove. It grows wild in hidden places and is the official national flower. There is a vast variety of other orchids; some say as many as one thousand species. Heliconias are abundant in Panama. This tree's enormous leaves have many different uses.

Breadfruit (left),
frangipani trees (center),
and the heliconia
plant (right) are
found in the lowlands.

The tropical rain forest of the lowlands occupies half the
country. The vegetation in this area includes a variety of species of
trees, many suitable for commercial forestry, particularly
mahogany, kapok, tagua, and cashew trees. Some other common
trees in Panama are the panama tree, the coruto, the frangipani,
the breadfruit tree, the cativo, the guarumo, the chumico
(sandpaper is made from its leaves), the calabash (for making
dishes and maracas), the orey, and, of course, palm trees, which
are used for wood, roofing, oil, and food (hearts of palm).
Poisonous plants like the diffenbachia can cause paralysis of the
mouth if any part of it is chewed or bitten. The beautiful oleander
plant provides the poison for arrows formerly used by the
Indians. In the islands of San Blas, bridge walkways have been
built in the rain forest, way up, so that botanists, zoologists, and
entomologists can conduct studies at a certain height. Only
Papua-New Guinea and Sulawesi (Celebes) have similar bridges.

Unusual animals that live in Panama are the white-faced monkey (far right), the margay (right), the jaguarundi (below right), and the anteater (below). This anteater is a baby clinging to its mother's back.

The variety of Panamanian animals is countless. One can find cougars; margays; jaguarundis; ocelots; small tigers, black and spotted, known as tigrillos; different varieties of monkeys, red, white-faced, titis, congo, and vampire; red, yellow, and black lions; Darién jaguars; armadillos; foxes; chungos; hedgehogs; anteaters; porcupines; nutrias; and coyotes.

Birds are abundant. More than eight hundred species are known. Panama shares birds of both continents and both seas. The unofficial national bird is the harpy eagle, which flies at a speed of forty or fifty miles (sixty-four to eighty kilometers) per hour to capture a monkey or a sloth with its sharp claws. It is found in the Darién area. The most frequently seen birds are royal eagles, swallows, quichiches, sparrows, hawks, owls, partridges,

A quetzal (left), blue morpho butterfly (top right), and a golden frog (bottom right)

flamingos, pelicans, jacksnipes, mockingbirds, woodpeckers, and vultures. The smallest bird is the hummingbird, which weighs .1 ounce (2.8 grams). Also found frequently is the quetzal in its resplendent plumage and the colorful blue or red-breasted tanagers.

Panama, like most tropical countries, except Cuba perhaps, has many dangerous snakes (some claim twenty-one species), like the coral snake, the bushmaster, the fer-de-lance, and the palm viper. There also are tree snakes and boa constrictors. A giant marine toad secretes highly poisonous venom, as does the golden frog whose poison could kill five hundred mice. Insects such as tarantulas, black widows, and scorpions are found here also. Butterflies are beautiful in Panama, the most striking species being the blue morpho.

The coastal waters of Panama are rich in marine life, including lobsters (above), manatees (above right), and barracuda (right).

With so much coastline, barracudas, sharks, manta rays, dolphins, manatees, crabs, shrimp (a source of great wealth for the Panamanian economy), lobster, and many other smaller fish as well as carey turtles (from which tortoiseshell comes) are found.

It is said that the true crocodiles are the ones found in Panama. They are large amphibious animals somewhat lizardlike in appearance. They are the last living link with the dinosaurs of prehistoric time. The only way to stop their snapping is to put a stick in their open mouths. Alligators belong to the same family, but they cannot live on land and must stay in the water.

To mention animals and plants found in a tropical country but to neglect to mention fruit would be impossible: sugarcane, mangoes, mameys, tamarind, cashews, honeyberries, star apples, custard apples, and of course, plantains and bananas—Panama's great export—are just a few of them. Clearly, Panama is a mecca for nature lovers.

Chapter 3

CUSTOMS AND CULTURE: INDIANS OF PANAMA

The original inhabitants of Panama were Indian tribes who were there when the Spaniards colonized the isthmus. Throughout the centuries they have, to a great extent, maintained their identity by keeping intact their languages, cultures, and way of life. The Indians have brought indigenous art to the country: the molas, made by the Cuna tribe, are among the better-known expressions of art in Latin America and art collectors from all over the world buy them.

It is probably because of the existence of the Indians of Panama, together with the canal, that so many tourists flock to this country.

Although, economically, they are not advanced, the Indians are an integral part of a country where so many races are represented. They are the most exotic of these races and a source of fascinating studies for anthropologists. Three main groups inhabit the Panamanian mainland, as well as the islands: the Cuna, the Chocó, and the Guaymí. There is also a smaller, lesser-known tribe called the Teribes in the northwestern region.

A Cuna woman wears the traditional gold nose ring of her culture.

It is believed that many centuries ago some Indian tribes left the Anahuac Plateau (Mexico) and migrated toward Central America. Aztec remains have been found in Panama. Some anthropologists and archaeologists also believe that other Indians left Peru and migrated north to Panama. This theory strengthens the statement that the Panamanian isthmus was and is the bridge where the cultures of south and north meet.

When the Spaniards colonized Panama, there was not much of an attempt to change the culture of the natives. The education they received was minimal. That is why their patterns of life have been preserved. It is only in recent times that some of the Indians have become "modernized," and only to a certain degree at that.

THE CUNA

Of the three groups of Indians found here, the Cuna are the best known, probably because of one of the art forms that they created—the art of mola making. The word *mola* means "cloth,"

A Cuna village nestled on one of the San Blas Islands

"dress," or even "blouse," but it actually refers to a panel of intricate hand appliqué work used by the Cuna women as part of their blouses.

The Cuna live on the northern shore of Panama, as well as in the hundreds of coral islands known as the Archipelago of Mulatas, or San Blas Islands. Some of the islands have names such as Wild Pig, Rabbit Island, or Big Orange. There are about 370 small islands in this archipelago and out of these, only about 55 are inhabited. Some island Cuna are more progressive than others and they maintain a unique culture of their own. The mainland Cuna are more primitive than their brothers of the islands. Most of them live on the banks of the Chucunaque and Bayano rivers. The Cuna's domain edges the region where Balboa led his men and founded the city of Santa María la Antigua del Darién, now disappeared. In it, too, was the now-extinct town of Acla where Balboa was beheaded.

Visitors who wish to go to visit the Cuna must fly to a nearby airport and then go by boat. The Cuna are friendly, courteous,

Left: Intricately designed molas are
made by the Cuna Indians. Right: An albino
Cuna Indian (fifth from left)

talkative (many speak Spanish besides their native tongue, Tule),
and eager to make a foreigner's stay pleasant.

The Cuna are short and strong. They speak rapidly,
accentuating the last syllables and interrupting in order to give
the listener a chance to agree, assent, or indicate understanding.
The Cuna women are no taller than 5 feet (1.5 meters) and weigh
70 to 80 pounds (32 to 36 kilograms). The men are from 5 feet to 5
feet 3 inches (1.5 to 1.6 meters). A heavy male will weigh about
110 pounds (50 kilograms). It is believed that the Cuna are the
smallest species of humans after the Pygmies. A very curious fact
is the high incidence of albinos among the Cuna. Albinos are
found all over the world, but the proportion is very high among
the Cuna. This phenomenon was already reported in 1699 by
Lionel Wafer, an Englishman who was both a surgeon and a
privateer and who visited the Cuna.

*Cuna youngsters (above) paddle their
boats near a cruise ship to greet
the tourists, and the women (right)
carry merchandise to sell at shipside.*

In 1925 the Cuna fought a war against the Panamanian
government. They proclaimed the Republic of Tule, but it was
shortlived. As a result of the uprising, it was later decided to give
the Cuna a territory of their own and a fair amount of autonomy.
The Cuna's territory is a strip of land called the Comarca de San
Blas, which goes from El Porvenir to Puerto Obaldía. The islands
off that shore complete the territory. The Comarca has a non-
Indian governor, but the Indians are allowed to vote. Outsiders
cannot buy land in the Comarca, but they can lease if they want to
build a hotel.

The land on the mainland strip is used for farming. It is also the
Cuna's burial ground. No one is buried on the islands. When an
Indian dies on an island, he or she is brought to the mainland to
be buried. In the old days, the islands were inhabited by black
runaway slaves called *cimarrones*.

Agriculture, fishing, and hunting are the Cuna's main means of livelihood. This is the men's responsibility, while women make molas. The Cuna use the slash-and-burn method of agriculture. In December the crops are cut, in March and April the roots of the crops are burned, and in May the land is sown. By the end of July the crops are usually ready for harvesting. Coffee, cocoa, corn, and tagus (ivory nuts) are the main crops. Coconuts are sold, mostly for coconut oil or for copra, the delicious inner spongelike center, in faraway markets such as Panama City, Colón, and Colombia in South America. This is an important source of income for the Cuna, and trade is a major part of their economy. The Cuna travel in small groups to reach the places where they will find buyers, usually Colombian sailors and traders.

The Cuna men go on distant fishing expeditions. They use fishing hooks, nets, and fishing corrals, or *empalizados*, which are small wooden traps in the water. They also fish at ebb tide with a sharp stick. The Cuna are experts at catching turtles and lobsters. All this fishing is done by the men, who return from fishing expeditions with smoked fish. Women and children fish only for shrimp and shellfish.

Hunting takes up a lot of the Cuna's time, and they are experts at it. The Cuna eat the animals they catch, such as ñeques, peccaries, wild pigs, iguanas, turkeys, and squirrels.

Cuna pottery is made by women. They make different household objects such as *braseros*, pans to hold hot coals to keep them warm at night, but the woodcraft and the basket weaving are the men's domain. Among the objects made from wood by men are kitchen utensils, such as mortars and, especially, the *piraguas* or *cayucos* (canoes) — boats that are used for transportation. These are hollowed-out tree trunks, usually

A Cuna family house (left) is used for sleeping, and a different structure is used for food preparation (above), where these women are cooking plantains.

mahogany or cedar, on which the Cuna often put sails and, nowadays, sometimes a little outboard motor.

A Cuna family's abode called *casa grande*, "large house," consists of a large room used for sleeping. Another separate structure is used for domestic chores and food preparation. This is also the dining room and it is called *casa del fuego*, or "fire house." In each village there also is the *casa de la chicha*, or "chicha house," where the Cuna gather for festivities and ceremonies. *Chicha* is an Indian drink made out of corn for everyday use and made from fermented sugarcane for special occasions. The *casa del congreso*, or "congress house," is used for important and political gatherings.

The Cuna have special houses (the equivalent of our hospitals) where the medicine men perform their special cures when someone is sick. The Cuna's medicine men are known as *nelés* or *innatuledis*. For healing purposes, the Cuna make therapeutic

These women pounding rice wear blouses made of molas. They also
have winis, beads that are strung in a pattern, wound around their arms
and legs. The woman on the right wears a necklace made of silver
coins. The black stripes on their noses are to keep away evil spirits.

medicine dolls called *nuchus*. Nuchus are placed next to the patient during the healing ceremonies. They also are used for good luck. They are usually made out of balsa wood in the shape of the human figure. They always have blue eyes, which are pins that can be taken out. Those Cuna Indians, who now are more educated, seek modern medical help.

In the Cuna society, there is also a prestigious wise figure called *kantule*, who is the historian and the priest. Sometimes a kantule becomes so prestigious that, besides his position acquired through study and dedication, he may be elected *sahila*, or "tribal chief." A kantule's hat is made out of straw with no top, and it is adorned all around with long, beautiful feathers.

The clothes worn by the Cuna men have been influenced by modern society. They usually wear shirts and pants. On rare occasions a man wears earrings. It is the women who still wear their indigenous costumes. The skirt consists of about 3 yards (2.7 meters) of cloth rolled around the waist and a mola blouse. A flat kerchief is worn on the head.

Cuna women's blouses are made with two mola panels seamed together at the sides and seamed to a yoke. The blouses have large puffy sleeves. Some molas are made for everyday use and some, more intricate ones, are worn on festive occasions. The molas are multicolored, with red a frequently used color. They take several months to complete. There may be as many as twelve different-colored cottons overlaid in appliqué or exposed through intricate reverse appliqué motifs. There are mostly geometrical designs in the molas, but the design often includes animals, flowers, plants, sea, sky, mythological scenes, and even modern-day objects such as airplanes.

The Cuna women are laden with jewelry: large earrings, gold breastplates, gold nose rings, and many gold rings on their

A close-up of the winis *and silver rings the Cuna wear. Gold as well as silver is made into elaborate jewelry (above right).*

fingers. Women also wear *winis* around their arms and legs. These are strung beads that form a pattern. They wear necklaces made out of silver coins picked up from sailors that come to San Blas. Women paint their cheeks with the bright red pollen from the achiote plant. They place a black stripe on their noses to keep the evil spirits away. Sap from the sapdur (or sabdur) tree is put on babies for protection against evil spirits.

The industry of mola making is one of the main sources of income for the Cuna Indians. People from all over the world come to the San Blas Islands looking for molas to buy. They can be used for blouses, to decorate a wall, to make cushions, or in any other creative fashion. Molas are taken by the Cuna to Panama City to be sold there. In their own homes, finished molas are often hidden to be kept away from the sun so the colors will not fade.

It is very much a part of a Cuna woman's tradition to be a good mola maker. If a girl who has been taught the art since childhood

Molas are sold for income and also are part of a Cuna girl's dowry.

is found not to be a good seamstress, there will be ceremonies where a medicine man will burn certain herbs to make her become one and, if that does not work, the girl's family has to hire a friend who sews well to come and do her work. Traditionally, a Cuna girl will bring about two dozen molas as part of her dowry when she marries. Most molas are 24 by 16 inches (60 by 40 centimeters).

When a girl reaches puberty, there is a "coming-out" party called *inna-nega*. Depending on the wealth of the family, anywhere from thirty to three hundred people will be invited. Families spend years saving for this three-day celebration. The occasion is one of great relevance: the girl is now a potential child bearer. She will be given her permanent name. She will have her hair cut. Prior to the feast, for many days, there will be hunting excursions to catch game and fishing expeditions to bring back fish. Sugarcane will be crushed to make chicha for drinking.

Before the ritual, the women in the family decide on the motif of the molas worn by the girl. They keep it a secret and they sit around for days sewing these beautiful molas. They will be worn, not only by the girl, but by all her female relatives. If it turns out to be a really attractive mola pattern, it will go around San Blas being copied and it will become the mola of the year.

When the feast begins, the kantules sit in the back of the chicha house and everyone chants for three days, telling the stories and mythology of the Cuna. The first and second day the women of the family serve the food and drinks, but on the third day, they join the party and everyone gets drunk. This is the only time when the Cuna drink. The most important moment in this festivity is when the honored girl gets her hair cut and gets her new name.

The Cuna society is monogamous and matrilineal—the inheritance comes down through the woman. Therefore, the birth of a daughter is welcome and celebrated. The woman is the holder of the land and of the jewelry that she wears and owns. In this respect the Cuna differ from many Indian societies where the women have few or no ownership rights. When two young people get married, the husband goes and lives with his wife's family. He works the land owned by her family so that the wife's family acquires a new work hand. He also fishes and hunts under the aegis of his father-in-law. In the islands, when a girl reaches marriageable age (between fourteen and seventeen years of age), the parents arrange the match with a boy who is usually seventeen to nineteen years old. Prior to the marriage, the inna-nega will have taken place. The attributes of feminine desirability are beauty, chastity, and domestic abilities. The boy will be a good candidate if he is strong and hard-working.

After the parents have arranged the marriage, the two youngsters meet, if they have not met before. If they like each other, they flirt with their eyes. One night, the boy's friends will catch him and drag him over to the girl's house where she awaits him sitting in a hammock. The boys throw their friend into the hammock. He usually jumps out and runs away and his friends bring him back. If he runs away three times, the marriage is off. If not, the young couple spend the night holding hands and talking. The marriage is consummated a few days later.

The young couple will live with the wife's parents. Only when her parents die will they build a new home of their own and the cycle will start again. The Cuna have large families. They are very affectionate with their children who are constantly being hugged, touched, and kissed. When a Cuna woman dies, her children are immediately taken over and cared for by her relatives and their families. If a married couple wants a divorce, the man simply puts his scanty belongings in a basket and goes home to his family.

Babies are first given their mother's milk. One month later they are given a banana drink. By the time they are ten months old, they eat solid food.

Little boys go naked until they are about five or seven years old, but little girls wear their native dresses with little mola blouses. When they are one month old, baby girls have their noses pierced and a coconut-soaked thread (to prevent infection) is inserted so that some days later they can wear a nose ring. The ring is changed as the child grows so that she wears a larger ring each time.

Older girls in the family take care of the smaller babies. They sing songs to them about their past, the family, and Cuna mythology.

The Cuna are not materialistic. They only want to take care of their basic needs. They are honest people. When strangers are invited to have a meal with a Cuna family, generally the man eats with the guests while the women eat elsewhere. Guests are given water to rinse their mouths after the meal, and they are supposed to make a lot of noise and splashing before spitting the water out.

In these modern times, many Cuna men leave their land to go and make a living elsewhere, at least for a few years. They often go to the cities of Colón or Panama City and work in the Canal Zone or as short-order cooks in restaurants. They also enlist on foreign ships in order to travel and get to see the world. More and more, the Cuna men are becoming trilingual, speaking Tule, Spanish, and English.

For centuries, there have been Catholic missionaries living in the San Blas Islands and some Cuna are Christians. Others—the majority—retain their own ancestral beliefs.

Slowly, the Cuna are becoming assimilated into modern life.

THE CHOCÓ

The Chocó are made up of Indians who live for the most part on the banks of rivers in the very lush and dense tropical jungle of the Darién region. They speak two languages: Embera and Wounaan. The vast majority of this tribe lives in Colombia, on the other side of the border from Panama. In their physical aspect, their culture and socio-economic structure, the Chocó are very similar to the tribes of Indians that inhabit the banks of the Amazon River.

The Chocó canoes (piraguas), made for river usage, are hollowed out in the middle and have platforms at each end used

Chocó Indians transporting plantain roots (above).
Chocó men and boys wear a guayuco, a loin cloth
that hangs from a thread worn around the waist.

for standing while throwing a harpoon for fishing. The Chocó use blow pipes and keep trophies that indicate victories over enemy tribes, such as skulls of enemies and necklaces made out of their teeth. In the past the Chocó took slaves and incorporated them into their group.

The Chocó are fairly tall and well-proportioned. Their hair is not quite so dark as other Indians' hair. The men usually wear nothing but a loin cloth called a *guayuco,* which hangs from a thread worn around the waist. They sometimes wear a multicolored shirt or a vest covered with coins but, more often than not, they go bare chested. For festivities, the Chocó wear an *ambura,* a hip hugger made of multicolored woven threads, and a chest plate made of many beads. Sometimes, a carved peccary tusk hangs from the chest plate. (A peccary is a mammal related to a pig.) The most important element worn on festive occasions is the silver-hammered jewelry: crowns, earrings, and bracelets. The Chocó also cover their faces and bodies with paint made from fruit.

*Chocó women wear beaded necklaces and
decorate their skin with paint made from fruit.
Chocó homes (above) are built on pilings
and access is gained by ladders.*

The women's clothing for festivities is simpler. They wear a multicolored piece of cloth, about 2 yards (1.8 meters) long, which is rolled around the hips and goes all the way to the knees. They go bare-breasted and only wear some minor necklaces.

The Chocó live in houses built on pilings so that they are quite high. The roof is usually cone shaped. There is practically no furniture inside. For the most part, the Chocó sit on the floor and sleep on straw mats. Each house has a mobile staircase or ladder used to climb up. The ladder is removed at night so animals cannot creep up.

Next to the house, one can usually find old piraguas—no longer good for navigating but used as nurseries for plants. Piragua making is one of the Chocó's great specialties. These are usually made out of cedar or yellow pine. The tree to be used for that purpose is cut during the last quarter of the moon because the Chocó believe that this will keep it free from termites. There is a

*Carving a canoe paddle (left) and drying
reeds (right) that will be used in basket weaving*

ceremony for launching a piragua to which friends and relatives
are invited. The piraguas constitute the main system of
transportation for the Chocó, since the area where they live has a
great number of rivers and streams.

Both men and women work in the field. They grow bananas,
corn, rice, and vegetables. The men hunt with bows and arrows
and spears. Their fishing is often done standing in their piraguas.

Arts and crafts among the Chocó are divided according to sex:
basket weaving and ceramics are women's activities while
woodcraft is left to the men. Woodcraft includes making cooking
utensils or walking sticks and carving ritual sculptures and altars
to their deities.

The Chocó constitute a patrilineal society where everything is
inherited through the men and the father is the main authority.
However, women are not left to occupy an inferior place. They
have property rights and are usually consulted by the husband
before making any decision that concerns the family.

When a young man decides he wants to marry a certain girl, he goes to her house and climbs up in order to be with her. If the girl accepts him, she scratches him with her nails. Marriage is monogamous.

The Chocó are great sportsmen. They ride horses very well, usually bareback. They are wonderful swimmers and extremely able underwater fishermen. They can catch and kill a fish with a machete as they swim. They like to wrestle and indulge in a particular form of this sport called *el lagarto*, the lizard. In the old days, they would hunt wild boars bare-handed.

When a Chocó Indian is sick, he tries to get cured through the use of medicinal plants, which are cultivated and grow around each house. Plants are used as laxatives, diuretics, sedatives, and disinfectants. However, when plants do not cure him, the Chocó will go to a *jabaina*, or medicine man, who will call upon the spirits.

The Chocó constitute a small but interesting and independent native group in Panama, since the majority of the tribe lives across the border in Colombia.

THE GUAYMÍ

The most numerous of the Panamanian Indian groups are the Guaymí who live in the western provinces of Chiriquí, Bocas del Toro, and Veraguas. Their everyday language is called *Morere*, or "language of the plains," but they all speak Spanish and are more advanced than the other groups. These are the Indians who before the Spaniards' arrival engraved symbols on mountain rocks and placed gold ornaments on their tombs. The Spaniards found them to be fierce warriors with expansionist tendencies.

Guaymí women wear sacklike dresses called do.

The Guaymí are tall and well shaped. They are graceful in their movements and quiet and refined in their manner. Their facial features are attractive. Women wear their hair long, braided, and adorned with ribbons and precious stones. Their dresses, called *do*, are lightweight sack dresses worn with a petticoat with interwoven purple threads. Men wear pants and shirts. They wear a type of ornament or jewelry called *chaquira*, which is a necklace of beads made from bones and shells (nowadays, they are made out of glass). The bones or glass are painted in many colors and geometrical designs. Chaquiras have become very popular with tourists. A bag of woven fiber called *chácara* is a multi-purpose object worn on the shoulder. The chácara is often used by men for carrying seeds to be sown. Women place their babies in it, instead, and carry them on their backs.

Guaymí at a duty-free shop on the Panama-Costa Rica border

Pottery and ceramics was one of the Guaymí's main crafts, but not so much nowadays.

The Guaymí's houses vary according to the region in which they live. The area is large and there are many differences in the terrain. In Bocas del Toro, where it rains often, houses are built on piles. In the Chiriquí region, houses are usually flat on the ground and mostly round in shape. The Guaymí often build a separate house strictly for cooking purposes. The Guaymí, like other Panamanian Indians, are very clean but often have foul-smelling pigs living in the lower level of their houses to keep away mosquitoes who cannot stand the odor. The houses have a second level, called a *jorón*, used as sleeping quarters as well as for keeping the grain dry for the next season. There are deer or cow skins on the floor to sleep on. Sometimes hammocks made out of vegetable fibers are hung there for sleeping purposes also.

The Guaymí's diet is not much different from the other groups. It consists of rice, bananas, corn, coconuts, yams, beets, spinach, beans, and fruits. They also hunt and eat tapirs, deer, and rabbits. Tobacco is cultivated by the Guaymí.

A Guaymí woman milking a cow

The Guaymí are polygamous. The men are allowed to have
many wives. Usually they do not have more than three and some
only have one. Wives are obtained through purchase or barter.
Women are considered inferior in the Guaymí society. Their
inheritance goes to the husband's closest relative when he dies.
Many Guaymí who have become Christians are, of course,
monogamous. Wedding celebrations are small family gatherings
where they drink *guarapo*, fermented sugarcane juice, and chicha.

In the Guaymí culture there is no rite of passage festivity when
a girl reaches puberty, as in the Cuna tradition. However there is
a mysterious ritual, called *guro*, when a boy reaches puberty. He is
taken into the jungle by the elders of the tribe who make him
undergo harsh tests to prove his mettle and his manhood. While
the ceremony is taking place, the elders chant.

Music is an important part of the Guaymí culture. They make
their own instruments: flutes and simple wind instruments called
drus and *kirakros* (made out of tiger's bone). They also make
instruments out of large seashells, which they call *churie*, and

A Guaymí mother and child

trumpets out of a cow's horn, which are called *nibi-croto*. Another instrument called *sera-kuato* is made out of a turtle's shell. Their drums, *mund-zuns*, are made out of wood and deer skin.

The Guaymí men, as well as women, paint their faces on festive occasions with different black or colored designs. They also file their incisor teeth into sharp points.

The most important festivity in the Guaymí culture is a celebration called *balsería*. This has a pre-Columbian origin and it is a game still played today, although it is so violent and brutal that many have tried to have it banned. Although it is officially outlawed, it still takes place. It is basically a jousting game played with tree logs or sticks called *balsos*. There are two aspects to it: the two tribes who meet to fight each other want to prove their manhood, and the celebration of the games is an excuse for all of them to get drunk.

The tribal chieftain of one group sends some emissaries to

another tribe challenging them to the fight. They take with them some strings called *quipus*, on which each day a knot is tied so that the days that must pass before the celebration can be counted. If the challenge is accepted, the quipus are kept.

Preparation for the balsería consists of making large amounts of chicha and guarapo for drinking and the choosing of an open field where the games will take place. There, open huts are built where the visitors will sleep while the games last.

When the celebration is about to begin, the opposing team arrives with their wives. They are all dressed up and wear multicolored plumed hats. They paint their faces and often have stuffed animals (tigers, pumas, anteaters) tied to their shoulders. They play their musical instruments constantly, making a terrible noise. They start drinking immediately.

The first night the Indians must keep watch on their balsos and never go to sleep. The next day the challenges, or duels, begin. When an Indian asks another if he is a man, the second one answers, "yes," and the fight begins. The sticks used are 6.5 feet (2 meters) long and the fighters use them to really hurt their opponents. The game is very violent and there are many who are injured and, sometimes, killed.

While the men are fighting with the sticks, the women who are also very drunk, often fight too. But they do it with their hands only, pulling each other's hair and punching each other with their fists. At the end of the balsería, the women sing a sad song of farewell and everyone goes home until the next celebration.

The Guaymí's lot is hard. Many live in poverty on reservations in the northern part of Panama. One could say that their fate has been somewhat similar to that of the Native Americans in the United States.

Chapter 4

CUSTOMS AND CULTURE: OTHER ETHNIC GROUPS

Panama is a country made up of many different ethnic groups. The result is that these many diverse influences have brought together varied forms of folklore. Panamanians are happy people who take every opportunity for a celebration.

DRESS AND JEWELRY

One of the features of Panamanian folklore that is internationally known is its national dress for women: the *pollera*. It is outstandingly beautiful and is worn by Panamanian ladies whenever there is a national celebration, at carnival time, or at special occasions such as weddings. The headpiece that goes with the pollera is called the *peineta*. The costumes are richly hand-embroidered and are quite expensive. Polleras are worn with pride and joy by Panamanian women.

The pollera, which literally means "hen cage," had its origins in the wide skirts and low-cut blouses brought from Spain in the early days of the colony. The Panamanian version of these dresses took something from the ones worn by Spanish ladies of different regions of Spain but, mostly, from the dresses worn in Valencia.

Opposite page: Polleras are worn with great pride and joy.

These dresses were worn in Panama at first by slave girls and working women. They have evolved into today's pollera, a modernized version of them. Different considerations—including the climate—have had to do with present-day polleras. This lovely dress has been worn by Panamanian women abroad. One Panamanian lady went to see the pope at the Vatican wearing her pollera. The pollera has been seen in Miss Universe and Miss World contests. It has been worn by members of Panamanian folk dance groups touring North America and Europe. The pollera *de gala* or *de lujo*, "gala" or "deluxe," is a distinguished and elegant costume that shows the taste of Panamanian women. It consists of hand-embroidered petticoats and underskirts, a full embroidered skirt, and an off-the-shoulder, highly embroidered blouse. The fine material is white and so are the laces, but the decorative embroidery can be of different colors. These and all other decorations are called *aderezos*. Sometimes a *rebozo*, or shawl, also is worn with the costume. There are many different versions of the pollera, depending on the region of Panama, or on whether the dresses are to be worn every day or for festivities. There even are some polleras for mourning worn in rural areas. The simpler versions are often a blouse, which is a little less ornate than that of the pollera de gala, known as *camisa montuna*, which is worn over a plain long cotton skirt.

The jewels worn with the pollera are very luxurious and when rich Panamanian girls wear the pollera de lujo they wear not only many gold, silver, or precious stone necklaces, but also lavish headgear. Panamanian gold and silversmiths, as well as pearl specialists, make beautiful jewelry.

Among the headgear worn with the pollera de gala, one finds *peines*, combs; *peinetones*, large combs in the shape of a tile; and

The headpiece worn with the pollera is called a peineta, *and is made of many different ornaments.*

pajuelas, small daggers with flowerlike decorations protruding from the blade. More important than anything else worn on the head are the *templeques*, ornaments that shake, said to be of Chinese origin. The *parches,* small square gold pieces adorned with a pearl, are worn close to the skin. Earrings are usually made in three parts that can be taken apart. All this jewelry gives a dazzling effect.

Panamanian men wear the *montuno* costume, which consists of a white embroidered shirt (the best comes from Ocu) worn over normal trousers, often white, and a *sombrero pintado*, a straw hat with black designs on it. Each province has a different design for the hat. These hats are meticulously handwoven from three different fibers that come from the leaf of the palm tree. Women in remote mountain areas of the Veraguas and Coclé provinces awaken at 4:00 A.M. to weave the hats until 8:00 A.M. because the

Tourists shopping for handwoven hats in the market

air, at that time, is heavy with humidity, giving the fiber a greater flexibility. During the day, the hat that is being made is wrapped in a damp cloth until worked upon again that night. Sometimes it takes as long as four months to make a hat. The famous Panama hat, strangely enough, is not made in Panama but in Ecuador, and it was called a Panama hat because it was brought there (like so many other things brought to the Crossroads of the World) in order to be sold.

There are other vestiges of olden times in costumes still worn today in Panama for different occasions. These include the *matinee*, a special blouse of French origin; the *basquiña*, a blouse with lace ornaments and a high collar; and the *chambra*, probably of French origin, too. A housecoat called *dama joven*, "young lady," is worn at home only. *Cutarras* are sandals that consist of a leather sole and thin leather straps woven together.

Left: Cuna woman playing a traditional pan pipe
Right: Cuna villagers perform a dance of their forefathers
for tourists who are visiting their island.

MUSIC AND DANCE

Music and dance are an important part of Panamanian life and, of all the dances, the *tamborito* is the best known and claims to be the national dance, while the *cumbia* and the *punto* also are popular. There are many versions of the tamborito, but in any of them we find a mixture of the different cultures that make up Panama. This dance had its origin in past centuries in the music played in European courts that, when transplanted to Panama, had native elements, in the theme and in the rhythm, added to it. The *bocana* and the *mejoranera* are five-stringed guitars used in Panama.

In Panamanian folklore, there are two distinct black influences: the Afro-Colonial and the Afro-Antillian (black workers who came to work on the railroad and the canal). Of the two, the strong

51

These congo dancers in Portobelo use a combination of African and Spanish steps.

influence on the local dances is from the African blacks that came as slaves. The dancers wear a great deal of gold and pearl jewelry, showing the native Indian influence. Composers of popular Panamanian music are many: Narciso Garay, Arturo Hassan, Avelino Muñoz, Alberto Galimany. Rubén Blades, so popular in the United States, is Panamanian. He is called the king of salsa. As to composers of classical music, Roque Cordero is the foremost.

FESTIVALS

Panama is a country of many festivals. Since it is a Roman Catholic country, most of the festivals are religious. Perhaps the main celebrations are the carnival festivities, the time to have fun before Lent begins. They take place the four days before Ash Wednesday. Many towns in Panama have carnival celebrations

*A religious procession beginning at the Cathedral of Penonomé (left)
and the revelry of the pre-Lenten carnival (right)*

and they vary from one to another. In the majority of them the celebration consists of *comparsas*, groups of people merrymaking, dancing, and playing instruments in the streets. Sometimes young boys throw water on the people dancing or singing. Wooden stages or tents for bands and performers are built near the beaches or harbors and, finally, on Ash Wednesday, after the last day of Carnival, people run to the beach for a ceremony called the burial of the sardine, and from there, they go to church.

Many other colorful feasts also take place in Panama. These are mainly processions where a well-loved statue of a saint, Christ, or the Madonna is carried on the shoulders of the people and venerated. The celebration held on the island of Taboga each July is famous. There are local boat races in honor of the patron saint of this island, and the statue of the saint is taken all around the island by boat.

Also famous is the procession of the three-hundred-year-old Christ in the old city of Portobelo where some penitents carry the statue on a platform and others walk behind it dressed in purple tunics. They take three steps forward and two back. This statue is particularly venerated by the many blacks who live in Colón.

Another religious procession is the one that takes place on the first Sunday in Lent near the town of Santiago de Veraguas, which is Jesús Nazareno de Atalaya. The faithful pray to the statue of Christ and promise gifts of jewels, money, and sacrifice if He will grant their wishes. It is said that many years ago the statue of Christ appeared in the town. When people tried to move it and carry it off to another town, the statue became very heavy and could not be moved.

LEGENDS AND STORIES

Panamanians have many lovely legends and stories that are told to children. One legend tells about a field near the town of Santiago de Veraguas. From the town, people would see a light on that field, but when they went there, there would be no light. People understood this to mean that a college to train teachers should be built there. The light that people saw, *la luz del llano*, symbolized the beacon of light that was to be education.

A story is also told of Belisario Porras, a famous Panamanian political leader, who was fleeing during a war because he was being followed in hot pursuit by his enemies. When he arrived at this same llano, where the light had been seen, he saw a very tall lady wearing the long ample skirt that peasant women wear. He asked to hide under the skirt and did, and when the enemy arrived, he could not be seen and thus he was saved.

Ruins of Old Panama are preserved in a park area just outside of modern Panama City.

COLONIAL REMNANTS

As to remnants of old colonial architecture, Panama offers many examples of it, some in ruins, some in beautiful condition. The country boasts the founding of some of the oldest towns on the American continent. These occurred shortly after the discovery by Bastidas and his companions. In most cases not much is left of these towns, but enough to show what Spanish colonial architecture was like.

The ruins of Santa María la Antigua del Darién, founded in 1510, can hardly be seen. This village's houses were mainly wood and disappeared when a terrible fire occurred, but one can still find partial ruins of brick houses, iron fragments, bullets, and Indian and Spanish pottery. The vestiges of an old cemetery can be found.

Panamá La Vieja, "Old Panama," as it is called now, was built in 1519. Its devastation in 1671 by the British pirate Henry Morgan

Modern skyscrapers dominate a panoramic view of Panama City (above).
In the old section of Panama City (below) there is much colonial architecture.

and its burning at the hands of the Spaniards themselves who did not want Morgan to profit, left little of what had been a fairly large town for its day. Morgan took 175 mule loads of booty. However, one can still see today some marvelous ruins of the old cathedral and some public buildings.

PANAMA CITY

Old Panama never recovered and the Spaniards built a new city two years later, five miles (eight kilometers) away from the old site. They wanted a better protected city so they chose a safer spot, a peninsula, and built a massive wall around it. This is Panama City, the capital, where one finds in *el casco viejo*, "the old section," old colonial houses with lovely balconies and a cathedral built in 1688 that has the highest towers in all of Central or South America, used as beacons for ships. The famous golden altar, painted to escape destruction by Morgan, is now in the church of San José. There are underground tunnels in the old section that are believed to have been built as a protection against pirate attacks.

In Panama City's old section there is a street called *Salsipuedes*, "Get out if you can." It is only two blocks long. Tradition has it that the name came from the fact that this street, located in Chinatown, was full of gambling houses where adventurers, shady characters, crooks, and rogues congregated. One never knew whether one could get out alive. Today this tiny street is full of *tenderetes*, "market stands." At the end of the street, there is a building that has balconies that look like peinetas, so people call the building La Pollera.

In the city of Panama City too, one finds a little park called

Left: The ruins of the Church of Santo Domingo and the flat arch Right: Apartments and hotels in an upper-class section of Panama City

Anayansi, next to the statue of Balboa. Anayansi was the daughter of an Indian chieftain and Balboa's mistress. The ruins of the church of Santo Domingo in the old section boast the old *arco chato*, "flat arch," that all tourists admire. It is called the impossible arch, because it subsists without a keystone or internal support—an unbelievable architectural feat.

When the United States decided to build the canal, there was controversy as to whether the site should be Nicaragua or Panama. The fact that the French had already done considerable work digging a canal in Panama seemed a good reason for doing it there. In addition, another item used to build a strong case for Panama was the argument that Nicaragua was subject to earthquakes while Panama was not. The proof was that the arco chato still stood after many centuries.

Just on top of Panama City is La Cresta. From here a magnificent panorama of the city can be admired. The residential

City buses (left) are painted by local artists and no two are alike. The Museum of the Panamanian Man (above) is devoted to the pre-Columbian history of the country.

areas close to the capital have many palatial homes. Buses in Panama are small vehicles called *chivas*, "goats," that dart around the city. Shopping is a wonderful experience here.

MUSEUM OF THE PANAMANIAN MAN

Of all the museums in Panama, the most outstanding one is the Museum of the Panamanian Man located in the heart of Panama City in what used to be the railway station. It provides the visitor with a complete overview of the country's history from the earliest times. The museum has assembled important historical, archaeological, ethnographical, and anthropological collections. In what used to be the canal zone, one can find a 25-foot (7.6-meter) topographical model of the canal, showing the entire length, the town sites, Thatcher Ferry Bridge, and the lock system. Within the old zone, one can visit Summit Gardens, a 300-acre (121 hectare)

garden that serves as an introduction to tropical flora.

The islands off the shore of Panama City—Contadora and Taboga—are tourist centers. Contadora often is used as an international summit center. It is here that the heads of state of several Latin American countries have met to discuss their common problems and have, therefore, been called the Contadora Group. The shah of Iran took refuge here for a while after he was deposed in 1979. There is another island called Coiba, which is used as a penal colony.

TOWNS FROM THE SIXTEENTH CENTURY

The oldest church in Panama is found in Natá, a city that was very important in the very early colonial times. The church was built in 1520 and is still in use. In the province of Coclé where Natá is, there is an extremely important archaeological site called Sitio Conte, where pre-Columbian vestiges can be seen. Here, among other things, magnificent pieces of Coclé gold jewels were found. They were made with a special method called the lost wax process. The desired shape is made of wax and covered with plaster or clay, with a few holes in it. The shape is heated and the wax melts and flows out the holes. Then melted gold is poured in, replacing the wax. When the gold hardens, the plaster or clay is broken, leaving the gold jewelry.

Portobelo, the Spanish Main's richest town, a town once famous for its fairs where wealthy merchants met, is believed to have been founded around 1580. It is now a poor, drowsy fishing village. Many lovely colonial ruins remain: San Fernando Fort, the old Customs House, several convents, churches, and hospitals, as well as the aqueduct, parts of old walls, and cannons. In the

Left: Taboga Island is a tourist center off the shore of Panama City.
Right: The ruins of Fort San Lorenzo near Portobelo

cathedral, the famous Black Christ statue is kept. The old fort of San Felipe Todo Fierro (St. Philip All Irons) was unfortunately torn down and dismantled by U.S. engineers to make a wall of contention for the city of Colón.

At the bottom of the sea, near a small island at the end of the bay where Portobelo was built, lies the body of Sir Francis Drake, the feared English pirate. He died of a fever and his men placed him in a lead casket and threw it into the sea. No one knows exactly where his casket is, but the legend has been passed down from generation to generation that it lies there.

Near Portobelo are the ruins of Fort San Lorenzo. This bastion located at the mouth of the Chagres River was once strategically located, built to stop the pirates and the buccaneers who constantly tried to ransack the country, yet it could not stop Henry Morgan and his men on their way to destroy Panama in 1671.

All around the coastline of Panama it is believed that galleons, still holding gold and other treasures, lie at the bottom of the sea waiting to be discovered.

LITERATURE

Panama's literature has its origins in the early chroniclers that came from Spain and wrote about Panama, its people, and its conquest and colonization. Basilio de Oviedo, Pedro de Anglería, and Antonio de Herrera were among the most noteworthy writers who recounted these early times. Hernando de la Cruz, a Jesuit priest, wrote excellent poetry in the early eighteenth century.

Printing was introduced in Panama in 1820 at the time of independence from Spain. Some early literary figures are Manuel J. de Ayala, writer and lawmaker; Victor de la Guardia, who wrote the first Panamanian play in the beginning of the eighteenth century; Sebastián López Ruiz, writer and physician; and political writer, Justo Arosemena. Martin Feuillet and Amelia Denis de Ycaza were romantic poets. Jerónimo de la Ossa wrote, among many other poems, the lyrics of the National Anthem. In the roster of Panamanian writers, poets, and essayists, are former President Ricardo J. Alfaro, Andreve, Batalla, Zoraida Díaz, María Olimpia de Obaldía, Juan A. Morales, Demetrio Korsi, Javier Laurenza, Octavio Méndez-Pereira, Leopoldo J. Arosemena, Rogelio Sinán, and Panama's greatest poet, Ricardo Miró.

Many literary contests take place in Panama, some for novels, others for essays or poetry. In the capital, there are theatrical productions, concerts, and ballets. More and more the provincial cities are developing their own cultural agenda. It is in Panama City that Dame Margot Fonteyn, a world-class British ballerina, who was married to a Panamanian, Roberto Arias, son of President Harmodio Arias, organized many ballet performances.

Panamanian painters, and there are many of them, usually

A Cuna Indian artist and his work (left) and artist Alfredo Sinclair (right) in his studio

choose the sea, country landscapes, and the pollera as subjects for their paintings. Some of the best-known painters are Manuel E. Amador, Sebastián Villalaz, Carolos Endara, Roberto Lewis, Rogelio Sinán, José G. Mora, and the best known of all—Juan M. Cedeño. The indigenous form of art, mola making, is the Cuna Indians' main contribution to Panamanian art.

Spanish is the official language of the country, but English is widely spoken because of the great number of North Americans who have lived here in connection with the canal and also because of the blacks that have come from the West Indies and have kept their language. There are newspapers published in both Spanish and English. Two main ones in Spanish have been *La Estrella de Panamá* and *El Panamá, América*.

RELIGION

Panama is a very cosmopolitan country because of its world trade and ships from all over the world passing through. Besides,

Cuna Indian schoolchildren

Panama is a country that has always been a melting pot of nationalities and diverse ethnic groups: Spanish, native Indians, blacks from Africa and from neighboring islands, Asians, French, Greek, Italians, and Jews (some are descendants of the old Spanish Sephardic Jews, some are Ashkenazis that left Europe in the 1930s, and others are Jews that left Algiers at the time of its independence).

The great majority of Panamanians are Roman Catholic. The Bishopric of Panama was the first one established on the American continent. The Catholic church has great influence in the country. There are, however, other religious groups in Panama: Protestants, Hindus, and Islamic congregations.

EDUCATION AND HEALTH

Panamanian children have a right to receive an education. Elementary schooling is compulsory and free for children from

The legislative building in Panama City

the ages of seven to fifteen. Secondary schooling is also free. The University of Panama is state run and the University of Santa María la Antigua is Roman Catholic. At the Technological University of Panama, students study engineering and high technology. The literacy rate in Panama is over 87 percent. Thanks to the ministry of health, health standards are among the highest in Latin America, a far cry from what it was when the canal was first being built. Life expectancy today is 72 years for men and 76 for women.

GOVERNMENT

Panama is a republic. It is made up of three governing branches: the executive, the legislative, and the judiciary. The executive branch is headed by the president and under him are two vice-presidents. They are elected for a period of four years. The ministers that form the Cabinet answer to the president. The legislative branch is made up of one house, the Assembly, and the judiciary branch encompasses the Supreme Court and other courts of justice in the land.

The national flag is red, white, and blue. It is made up of four rectangles, in two of which a star is placed. The national anthem was composed by Santos Jorge and Jerónimo de la Ossa.

FOOD

Panama has been blessed with a bountiful nature that provides its inhabitants with a great variety of delicious edibles whether they be fish, fowl, deer, or other similar animals, vegetables, or fruit. It is the Panamanian people, however, who have created an excellent cuisine that utilizes what Mother Nature has provided.

Fish and seafood are abundant and are prepared in many ways. Some specialties include *bolitas de pescado*, "fish balls," made of Panama's number-one fish *corvina*, "conger." They are breaded and fried. *Ceviche*, common to other Latin American countries, is delicious. The fish and shellfish are marinated overnight in lemon juice and spices and eaten raw, although the marinade "cooks" the fish. *Sancocho de mariscos* is a seafood stew that includes oysters and shrimp. Panamanian waters offer the inhabitants of the country an enormous variety of fish. There are marlins, red snapper, shad, giltheads, sea bass, and haddock. Shrimp and lobster are first-class.

Some local meat dishes are *sancocho de gallina*, "chicken stew," or *sancocho de carne*, "meat stew." *Tamal panameño* is made from yellow corn with pork, chicken, raisins, and cilantro, and wrapped

A Cuna woman preparing the evening meal

in *bijao* leaves (a smaller version of the banana leaf). Roasted iguana with rum sauce is a delicacy, and *carimañolas* is a typical dish consisting of yucca paste to which meat (or sometimes shrimp) is added. It is shaped into a cylinder and fried. Corn tortillas differ from the Mexican ones as they are thick and fried.

Chicharrones, fried pork rinds, are typical also. *Arroz con pollo*, chicken with rice, is a dish served frequently. Beans of different kinds are eaten. *Pelotitas de maíz* are ground corn balls. *Empanadas* are a type of crescent-shaped cakes that are filled with meat, chicken, or sweets. The *guacho* is another form of stew that is more liquid and contains many different ingredients. It is an everyday dish. The United Nations made a study that proved that the guacho is one of the most complete and nutritional dishes one can eat.

Besides the many green vegetables that are common to most countries in the world, in Panama one finds otoe, yucca, green papayas, and corn. The variety of fruit is enormous. Particularly popular besides bananas from Bocas del Toro or Darién are pineapples from Taboga Island, red papaya from Arraigau, water

Left: Bananas and limes for sale
in a market
Right: A Cuna woman strips corn
from the cob to sell with other grains.

from green coconuts from San Blas, as well as mangoes, cashews, guanábanas, mameys, nísperos, caimitos, mamoncillos, tamarinds, avocados, jobos, breadfruit, quince, watermelon, citrus fruits, pitaya, and cumba, to mention just a few. Strawberries, not usually found in the tropics, grow in the cool, mountainous climate of Chiriquí.

Panamanians are very fond of sweets and desserts. The best known is *sopa borracha*, "drunken soup," a pound cake on which sugar syrup, cloves, cinnamon, raisins, rum or brandy, and silver decorations are poured. If whipped cream is added too — for weddings and special occasions — it is called *sopa de gloria*, "glorious soup." *Manjar blanco* and rice with coconut or mangoes, as well as with *guandús* (gungo beans), are typical. Another popular dessert is *resbaladera*, made of rice, milk, sugar, cinnamon, and vanilla.

As for drinks, chicha is preferred all over the country and *chicheme* is a fruit drink to which sugar, milk, and vanilla are

Children wait to get the last bit of coconut from the sheil after this woman has removed the milk and the meat.

added. Panamanian rum is very popular, as is *seco herrerano*, a type of Panamanian tequila. Beer is brewed locally.

SPORTS

Panama is a mecca for sports. The climate is favorable for outdoor sports, since practice can take place outdoors all year round. All horse sports are popular. People like to ride and they particularly enjoy horse races. There have always been many excellent Panamanian jockeys who have ridden in the United States in the Kentucky Derby and other major races. Some of the jockeys are Jorge Velázquez, Laffit Pincay, Jr., Manuel Icaza, and Braulio Baeza.

Fishing is a very popular sport. Deep-sea fishing is done in both oceans where huge sailfish, blue and black marlin, tuna, swordfish, and barracuda are caught. Amateur fishermen from all over the world go to the Piñas Bay Club or the Tropic Star Lodge

A sandy beach on Taboga Island draws sunbathers.

for excellent game fishing. Scuba diving—the best is in Bocas del Toro—is a popular sport, as well as sailing.

But of all the sports that thrill Panamanians, baseball is definitely number one. Panamanians love to play it and they love to watch it. They follow the World Series closely. Soccer is also played in Panama, though not half as much as baseball. Rod Carew is probably the best known of all Panamanian ball players.

There are many public beaches in Panama so that everyone can go swimming, and it is interesting to find sand of many different colors from white to beige, to black, to grey, to greenish black. Panamanians also swim in the many rivers that are found in the country.

A family from the mountains above Boquete (above) and a young girl from Portobelo with a baby coati (right)

Cock fights, though a spectator game more than a sport, are very popular in Panama, as is boxing. There have been several world class Panamanian boxers in the history of the sport. Roberto (*Mano de Piedra*, "Stone Hand") Durán is a present-day champion, and Hilario Zapata, Eusebio Pedrosa, and Ismael Laguna are well known also.

Panama is a very family-oriented society, one where mothers have an important role and place. Some observers say that here Mother's Day is almost as important as Christmas. Panamanians are warm, affectionate, extroverted people who enjoy life.

Rodrigo de Bastidas (inset) arrived in Panama in 1501 searching
for gold. The Spaniards built a mule trail (above) across the isthmus
that was used to transport Inca treasures found in South America.

Chapter 5

ABUNDANCE OF FISH

Experts in Central America agree that the word *Panama* meant "the land where fish are plentiful" in an Indian dialect. The Indians that inhabited this strip connecting North and South America had come there from other parts of the continent long before the Spanish conquistadors arrived. It is believed that the Maya, the Nashua, the Caribs, and the Chibchas were the original settlers. By the time the Spaniards arrived, it is said that there were seventy-nine groups of Indians on the isthmus.

FIRST EUROPEAN VISIT TO PANAMA

Rodrigo de Bastidas was a scribe from Seville who was anxious to become rich. He set sail in October 1500 with two ships. With Bastidas were his pilot, Juan de la Cosa, an experienced navigator, and Vasco Núñez de Balboa, an adventurer who also sought fame and fortune. They reached the mainland in 1501 and explored the coast and islands of San Blas. Bastidas's ships were in terrible condition; the wood had rotted. This forced the group to go back to La Hispaniola (present-day Santo Domingo) and eventually, back to Spain. But Balboa chose to stay in La Hispaniola.

Christopher Columbus thought the area where he landed was so beautiful he called it Portobelo, *"beautiful port."*

COLUMBUS

A year later, in 1502, Columbus left Spain on his fourth and last voyage to the New World. The main purpose of his trip was to find the waterway through which he could pass and go on to India. He landed in what is now Honduras and continued down the coast of Central America, arriving finally at the isthmus region. Part of this coastline was named *Veraguas,* "to see waters." Here were mines of precious metals that were to yield great riches. To this day, the descendants of Columbus in Spain boast the title of dukes of Veraguas.

Arriving at a site that was later to become a bustling port, Columbus was so struck by its natural beauty that he called it *Portobelo,* "beautiful port." In his letters, Columbus wrote about the natural beauty of the area. He also wrote about his amazement at the great variety of animals, such as peccaries, pumas, and wild turkeys, which were "very large hens whose feathers are like wool." Columbus did some bartering with the Indians who gave him magnificent gold necklaces. The Indians talked about a Southern Sea, later discovered by Balboa.

The first settlement of the area was called Santa María de Belén. It did not last because the Indians destroyed it. Columbus saw the famous Chagres River and called it "River of the Alligators." After exploring a good part of the Atlantic coast and not finding the passageway to the Indies, Columbus, already ill, sailed back to Spain. He died in 1506.

SPAIN FIGHTS FOR CONTROL

The Spanish crown decided to send two conquistadors to govern the newly discovered land, dividing the territory into New Andalucía, the northern coast of present-day Colombia, under the command of Alonso de Ojeda, and Golden Castille (present-day Panama), governed by Diego de Nicuesa. The conquest of the territory was no easy feat. The native Indians were, for the most part, quite hostile. Heavy fighting took place as the Spaniards tried to advance and conquer. When in combat, the Indians used the bloodied shirts of the Spaniards as their banners.

The conquistadors' situation was very bad, and Nicuesa decided to abandon the territory, leaving Francisco Pizarro in charge. Pizarro was the man who was later to conquer Peru and its fabulous riches.

Meanwhile, the king of Spain ordered Martín Fernandez de Enciso to go and rescue the colonizers for whose fate he feared. Enciso set sail from La Hispaniola. Aboard his ship came a stowaway who, once discovered, managed to survive and escape the normal punishment for stowaways, which was to be thrown into the sea. The man was Balboa, who was intent on finding the Southern Sea mentioned by the Indians. Balboa was thirty-six years old and eager to escape his creditors in La Hispaniola where he had been farming. Red-headed Balboa was a natural and fearless leader. He fought hard when he had to fight, but he also managed to befriend some of the Indians. Balboa was even given the daughter of one of the Indian chieftains in marriage.

Following Balboa's advice, Enciso founded the first town of Tierra Firme, Santa María la Antigua del Darién, in 1510. This was the first sizable Christian settlement in the Americas and the first municipal government of the continent.

Balboa rebelled against Governor Nicuesa. Following a plebiscite, with the help of one of his followers, Samudio, Balboa named himself chief mayor. Balboa became sole ruler of the area.

After a while, Balboa formed an army of 190 Spaniards, some Indians, and many *alanos*, fierce dogs often used during the conquest of the Americas. The army trekked across the jungle of Darién. Panquiaco, the son of an Indian chieftain, gave Balboa 4,000 ounces (113,400 grams) of gold and told him to go beyond the mountain to find the Southern Sea. When Balboa reached the high peak of Pirre on September 25, 1513, he was astonished. He saw a huge body of water, the Southern Sea, which was later to become known as the Pacific Ocean. The group sang a hymn of thanksgiving and built a cross from a tree, which they embedded in the mountain after inscribing the names of the Spanish sovereigns on the barks of neighboring trees. Balboa quickly continued the descent to the waters of the sea. He waded in the waters and officially took possession of the sea in the name of the king of Spain.

Balboa then continued his travels along the southern coast. He met Tamaco, an Indian chieftain who befriended him and gave him gifts of gold and pearls. One pearl was so large that it was

Balboa taking possession of the Pacific Ocean for Spain

said to be the size of an egg. The Spaniards were astonished to see that the oars that the Indians used for their canoes were inlaid with pearls. Balboa called the islands there the "Archipelago of the Pearls." He returned to Santa María la Antigua loaded with riches and sent word to the king of Spain about his discovery.

THE SEARCH FOR GOLD

When the news of the discovery reached the old world, imagination ran wild and unbelievable tales were told. There were legends about an Indian chieftain who bathed in gold powder. The search for gold was moved from the Caribbean, where there was little of this precious metal, to the Darién region. This area became the magnet to which all fortune seekers were drawn. Even the hardships of the dense jungle, the poisoned arrows, the alligators, and the marches could not stop the men who were lured by the gold of this region. The discovery of the Pacific became one of the main feats of mankind, told and retold for centuries to come. The chroniclers of the time—Oviedo, Anglería, and others—have left accounts of this great happening.

PEDRARIAS

After his discovery, Balboa dispatched an envoy to the king of Spain bringing one-fifth of the gold collected and recounting the discovery of the Southern Sea (Pacific). Balboa asked to be made governor of Golden Castille, but the king had already sent a new governor. Shortly thereafter the new governor, Pedro Arias Dávila, known as Pedrarias, came with many ships and men. He was nicknamed "The Tiger of the Isthmus."

Strong antagonism and hostility grew between the two men, created by the jealousy Pedrarias felt toward Balboa. When Balboa realized that Pedrarias was not going to allow him to continue his exploration of the Pacific Ocean, he sent a friend to La Hispaniola to seek more men. Pedrarias found out and arrested Balboa. After a reconciliation, Balboa was allowed to continue his expedition. But in 1519, Pedrarias had Balboa brought to the town of Acla, where he had him beheaded in the village square on trumped-up charges.

Although cruel and unfair, Pedrarias was a good administrator who conquered and colonized the Isthmus of Panama. He founded cities, including Panama in 1519, and structured his territory according to the laws and regulations of Spain. He organized the Catholic religion according to the mandates of the church and squelched any rebellions on the part of the Indians. Pedrarias made it a point to *again* take possession of the Pacific

Ocean in the name of the king of Spain, trying in this manner to obliterate Balboa's accomplishment.

A PLACE OF PASSAGE

The region's riches and geography made Panama a meeting place as well as a place of passage for the whole world. The town of Nombre de Dios was a bustling port for trade. Panama became the choice starting point for expeditions and conquests. It was from Panama that Pizarro left to conquer the Inca Empire in Peru.

The next centuries did not bring great changes to Panama. The Indians were dying out and the Spaniards needed laborers. Black slaves were brought to work in the mines and to till the land. The process of colonization continued. Plants and animals from Europe were introduced. Huge tracts of land—what were later to be called *latifundios*, or very large land holdings—were handed out to the colonizers. The *encomienda* system was established whereby each Spaniard had a number of Indians put under his care. It was the Spaniard's responsibility to make the Indians work and to teach them Christianity. In 1538, Panama had been chosen as the seat of one of the main courts of justice in America, the *audiencia*. But because the country lost importance, the court was abolished in 1751. The focus was shifted from Panama to Peru because of the discovery of great riches in Peru.

COLONIAL PANAMA

The city of *Panamá La Vieja*, "Old Panama," grew slowly after it was founded. It was dependent on the arrival of ships from Spain or from the south. There were better ports that vied for first place

In the 1690s Old Panama (left) was attacked by pirates. One of the early pirates was an Englishman, Sir Francis Drake (right).

in importance, such as Cartagena de Indias (now in Colombia). The British and French pirates who came and went throughout the Spanish Main, landed frequently on the mainland. Among the early ones, Sir Francis Drake, John Hawkins, and Francis l'Olonnois were most famous. But it was Henry Morgan, the English pirate, who in 1699 took over Portobelo and besieged Old Panama.

Old Panama had various convents, churches, a cathedral that was the seat of the first diocese in the American continent, a general import office, and one thousand residential houses. When Morgan arrived with fifteen hundred buccaneers, the Spaniards were not able to defend the city. They burned it rather than hand it over to the pirate. A famous gold altar of great worth was painted brown to resemble wood. The pirates were totally fooled and did not steal it. This altar still exists in its original form and can be seen in a church in Panama City. Two years later, a new city of Panama was built on a site where it could be better defended, and forts and fortifications were built around it.

Henry Morgan, the pirate (left), and Edward Vernon, the admiral

Among the interesting happenings in the early colonial days of
Panama were the Portobelo fairs. This was a yearly event of great
importance. For forty days, the fairs were held and merchants
gathered to sell or trade their goods. Galleons came to collect the
treasures of gold, silver, and pearls. (More than thirteen hundred
ships were counted once in the harbor of Portobelo.) Then the
population rejoiced and celebrated. After the hustle and bustle of
the fair came what was known as the *tiempo muerto*, "dead time,"
until the following fair.

In 1739, during a war between Spain and England, known as
the War of Jenkins' Ear, Admiral Edward Vernon of the British
navy took Portobelo and practically destroyed it. This was a major
victory for England. Portobelo was never the same and the fairs
were no more. It was then that contraband was established as a
form of illicit trading that brought great riches to those involved.
It took away funds from the official customs houses. It is believed
that during colonial times in Panama, the volume of trade done
through contraband was greater than that of legal commerce, and
there was little that the Spanish government could do about it.

Life went on for several centuries in Panama without major
changes until the beginning of the nineteenth century, when the

Simón Bolívar fought for independence for Latin American countries.

winds of revolution followed the desire for independence of most Latin Americans. The main forger of independence was Simón Bolívar of Venezuela. A new country called Gran Colombia was formed. It included the vast territory of northwestern South America and it encompassed the Isthmus of Panama.

ALMOST INDEPENDENT

Panama became independent from Spain in 1821, but became a province of Colombia. This was accomplished without any bloodshed. Panama felt that being united to Colombia would give it protection from a possible attack from Spain. Panama also felt that the connection with Colombia would help its economy. Also, there existed, at the time, a sentiment of Latin American solidarity as well as an unbounded admiration for Bolívar, who has been called the Liberator of America.

An important event that took place in Panama during the nineteenth century was the Congress of Panama in 1826. Bolívar, the Liberator, had always dreamed of a united Latin America, with all the Spanish-speaking countries forming a confederation or community of nations. For this purpose Bolívar called a congress. Delegates from the different countries attended. But the mission of the congress never was realized.

The seventy-five years in which Panama was united to Colombia proved to be disastrous. Colombia did not foster Panama's agriculture, the cattle industry, or any other industry. There were several attempts to separate from Colombia between 1830 and 1840. In 1855, Dr. Justo Arosemena, one of Panama's great leaders and statesmen, established the Federal State of the Isthmus, which granted many concessions to the area. During the time when Panama was a federal state, there were some border problems with Costa Rica concerning the establishment of the line of demarcation between the two countries. However, all in all, the establishment of this federal state gave greater stability and many economic improvements to the isthmus and led eventually to the total severance of ties with Colombia.

A war called the War of the Thousand Days started in March 1900 between Liberals and Conservatives. The former were led by Dr. Belisario Porras. The war brought misery and desolation to the isthmus. It ended in 1903 when the Colombian government asked the United States to intervene and a peace treaty was signed on board the United States battleship *Wisconsin*. The main reason for the United States facilitating the end of the war was its interest in building a canal through the isthmus for navigation from the Atlantic to the Pacific.

The Gatún Locks in the Panama Canal can be raised and lowered in three steps. Above: The ship passing through has been elevated by the water in the lock. Below: The locks work independently. Ships enter at sea level and must be raised about 85 feet (26 meters), the level of Gatún Lake. Exiting ships are lowered by the locks.

Chapter 6

THE PANAMA CANAL

A few years after the discovery and conquest of the isthmus, Spain had already thought of dividing this narrow strip of land that separated the Atlantic and the Pacific. Balboa first conceived the idea of linking the two oceans through a water passage. Hernán Cortés considered this idea as something even more valuable than his own conquest of Mexico. Alvaro de Saavedra drew up plans for a waterway either across the Darién or through Nicaragua. Without a waterway, ships had to go all the way to the southernmost tip of the South American continent and circle Cape Horn.

In 1524, the Emperor Charles V of Spain asked Antonio Galván and later Pascual de Andagoya to look into this possibility. An eighteenth-century chronicler writes that a priest of the town of Novita had built a canal between the two coasts whereby, during the rainy season, small boats carrying cocoa could travel. This was the "ancestor" of the canal. In the early nineteenth century, Bolívar also talked about it. At the Congress of Panama of 1826, the United States made known its interest in having a canal built.

CLAYTON-BULWER TREATY

In 1835, the United States Senate presented a resolution that spoke of a canal that would offer free transit to all the nations by means of a toll payment in order to compensate those who would build it. A few years later Great Britain and the United States signed the Clayton-Bulwer Treaty whereby neither nation would occupy or colonize any part of Central America. They also would protect any means of communication going through the isthmus, whether a projected canal were to be built in Panama or in Nicaragua.

It was this very agreement that made the construction of the Panama Railroad by a group of North American engineers in the 1850s possible. The Gold Rush of California and the need to transport the precious metal to the East Coast, spurred this most difficult construction made at great costs of human lives, because of epidemics, and of dollars.

Years later, in 1901, the Clayton-Bulwer Treaty between the two great powers was to be abrogated and replaced by the Hay-Pauceforte Treaty, by which Great Britain gave up any claim.

FRANCE TAKES ACTION

In the meantime, the nation that acted and moved into action regarding the actual building of the canal was France. The French had built, shortly before, the Suez Canal in Egypt. The man who had been responsible for it was Count Ferdinand de Lesseps, an able man who had great credibility. In 1876, a descendant of Napoléon Bonaparte's brother, Lucien Napoléon Bonaparte Wyse, signed a treaty with Colombia that enabled him and a group of

Terrible landslides occurred when workers tried to dig the Culebra Cut, now called the Gaillard Cut. Although Ferdinand de Lesseps (inset) built the Suez Canal, his work on the Panama Canal was a disaster.

Frenchmen to perform a feasibility study for the building of a canal in the isthmus. A further treaty signed by the same parties in 1878 was then deeded by Wyse to the Compagnie Universelle du Canal Interocéanique headed by de Lesseps.

This company represented powerful vested interests of French capital, as well as the enthusiastic support of the whole French nation. The actual excavation work for a sea-level canal without locks and boasting a 3.7-mile (6-kilometer) tunnel began in 1880. Many people came from France to join in the excavation. Tremendous difficulties were encountered. The terrain ranged from marshes to jungles to moving land. The climate was tropical and the excavators caught yellow fever and malaria. All this, together with very poor administration of funds, as well as graft and greed on the part of the administrators, led to total disaster. The company was dissolved and a new one reorganized under the name of Compagnie Nouvelle du Canal de Panama.

But things went from bad to worse and eventually the bankruptcy and collapse of this company also occurred. The French government was nearly toppled because of the so-called "Panamanian Scandal," which rocked the very backbone of the French nation. In retrospect, one could say that the main reasons for the French failure in Panama were that the engineers underestimated the job based on the simpler job they had done in Suez. Their insistence on building a sea-level canal rather than one with locks, their inability to cope with the health problems caused by disease, and financial scandals took their toll.

THE HAY-HERRÁN TREATY

But France's loss was the United States's gain. Here was the golden opportunity the United States had been waiting for and indeed it was seized. On January 22, 1903, the United States and Colombia signed the Hay-Herrán Treaty by virtue of which the canal work would revert to the United States. However, the treaty was rejected by the Colombian Congress as unfair to Colombia. President Theodore Roosevelt sent battleships to the isthmus coast. The Panamanians began negotiating a future canal treaty. A few days later, Panamanian independence was declared.

THE HAY-BUNAU-VARILLA TREATY

The United States recognized the new nation and shortly thereafter the Hay-Bunau-Varilla negotiations began. This treaty was signed in Washington in 1903. Bunau-Varilla was a Frenchman who was an important shareholder of the French canal company and was anxious to sell. The newly founded nation of Panama, whose leaders were not expert negotiators, knowing that Bunau-Varilla had political connections in Washington, gave him the power to negotiate the treaty. Before anyone from Panama could arrive in Washington, Bunau-Varilla had signed a treaty that was very beneficial to the United States but did not take into account Panamanian interests.

United States Secretary of State John Hay himself was to say later that the treaty, which had been drawn up in haste, without enough study or preparation, was most advantageous for the United States but not so for Panama. Panama was never reconciled to having to give up its sovereignty of the Canal Zone. The United States paid $40 million to the French company for the right to take over their work and a yearly $250,000 as long as the treaty existed, plus the right to build on its territory and to use a strip of land five-miles (eight-kilometers) wide on each side of the canal called the Canal Zone. At the same time the United States was guaranteeing the independence of Panama. Years later, the United States signed a treaty with Colombia in which they apologized for what had happened and gave Colombia special prerogatives in the use of the canal and a payment of $25 million. In 1904, the Canal Zone was in fact transferred to United States jurisdiction.

YELLOW FEVER EPIDEMIC

The task ahead of the United States team was not an easy one. The first decision was to change the original plan and to build a canal with locks, which made the task much more feasible. Then came the enormous challenge of trying to eradicate the yellow fever epidemic. In 1881, a Cuban doctor, Carlos Finlay, had

Dr. Walter Reed (above left),
Dr. William Gorgas (above center),
and Dr. Carlos Finlay (right).
Far right: The canal workers that these
doctors protected from yellow fever

discovered that this dread disease was transmitted through a mosquito. Dr. Walter Reed, of the United States army, had done away with yellow fever in Cuba by a massive attack on this insect. One of Dr. Reed's followers, Dr. William Gorgas, was in charge of doing the same in Panama. He initiated a comprehensive program of drainage, spraying, trash cleanup, and the development of a sewage system. He was enormously successful, so that by the time the actual work on the canal began, the area was free from disease. The United States also built houses for the work force, which had to be imported because Panama lacked available labor. The skilled workers came mostly from the United States and the unskilled workers from the West Indies and Europe.

AN INTEROCEAN WATERWAY

The canal, as it was built by United States engineers, led first by chief engineer John F. Stevens and then by Colonel George W.

George W. Goethals

John F. Stevens

Construction of the Miraflores Locks (above) in 1913
and the Pedro Miguel Locks (right) in 1910

Goethals of the United States army engineers corps, has been
described as an interoceanic waterway that connects the Atlantic
and the Pacific oceans through the Isthmus of Panama by means
of a lock system. The original elevation was 312 feet (95 meters)
above sea level where it crosses the continental divide. This
waterway is 50 miles (80 kilometers) from the deep waters of the
Caribbean to the deep waters of the Pacific Ocean. The town
located at the northern end of the canal is Cristóbal, named after
Christopher (Cristóbal) Columbus. At the southern end is Balboa.

   The canal was cut through one of the narrowest places and at
one of the lowest saddles of the long isthmus that connects the
two continents. A ship is raised or lowered 85 feet (26 meters) in
a continuous flight of three steps at Gatún Locks. The length of
Gatún Locks is 1.2 miles (1.9 kilometers). Gatún Lake, through
which the ships travel for 23.5 miles (38 kilometers) from Gatún
Locks to the northern end of Gaillard Cut, is one of the largest
man-made bodies of water in the world. It was formed by
building an earth dam across the famous Chagres River. Then an
enormous cut had to be made through the mountains at a place

The Madden Dam (left) was built in 1935. The Pedro Miguel Locks (right) are near the Pacific Ocean side of the canal.

known as *Culebra*, "snake." Culebra Cut was the greatest obstacle encountered by the builders of the canal. There were terrible landslides to contend with and the land extracted was said to have equaled that needed to make a pyramid 892-feet (272-meters) high. The worst landslide was called *cucaracha*, "cockroach." Because of the landslides, weeks of work were wasted. These slides occurred not only during construction but even after the canal was opened, so that it had to be closed down for six months for repair.

Building the canal was the largest excavation in history, which was directed by an engineer named David DuBose Gaillard, whose name was eventually given to the passage. Since then, the Gaillard Cut has had to be widened from a width of 300 feet (91 meters) to one of 500 feet (152 meters). Another improvement has been the construction of the Madden Dam in 1935. On the other side more locks, the Pedro Miguel and the Miraflores locks, help lower the ships to sea level and out to the Pacific.

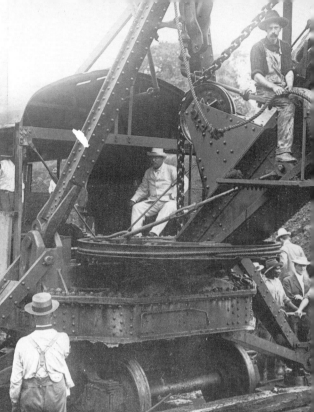

Both William Howard Taft (above)
and Theodore Roosevelt (right)
visited the canal when it
was under construction.

The project that was undertaken and completed by the United States is one of the most extraordinary feats of engineering ever accomplished, and it has been recognized as such all over the world. British historian James Boyce called it "the greatest liberty man has ever taken with nature." The United States had planned and executed this masterpiece with technical knowledge, ingenuity, practicality, and organization. The U.S. people followed the building of the canal with excitement. This was one of the great sagas of U.S. history. Even Presidents Theodore Roosevelt and William Howard Taft went to inspect the site. This enormous undertaking was finally finished in 1914, and on the 15th of August of that year it was officially inaugurated. The cost of building this waterway was approximately $387 million. The Panama Canal has the distinction of being the only United States government project finished ahead of schedule and under budget. It was hardly touched by scandal or corruption.

The Bridge of the Americas

LATER CANAL IMPROVEMENTS

A number of major improvements to the canal have been made since the time of initial construction. Some of these are the Madden Dam that was built on the upper Chagres River, the displacement of the old-fashioned towing locomotives with modern ones, and the building of a state-of-the-art bridge that spans the Pacific entrance to the canal and is called the Bridge of the Americas. In 1915, a Panama-Pacific International Exposition was held in San Francisco celebrating the opening of the Panama Canal as well as the rebirth of the city of San Francisco after the earthquake and fire of 1906.

OPENING THE CANAL

For Panama the opening of the canal meant a great boon to its economy. It has probably earned from it about $200 million a

The first ship to pass through the Panama Canal was the S.S. Ancón.

year in direct or indirect income. But what was always a thorn in
Panama's side was the lack of control that it had on the canal.
Unlike other countries who own a great resource located on their
land, Panamanians did not exercise sovereignty over the canal.
They could not tax it, license it, or direct it, since it did not belong
to them. This was the cause of great resentment on the part of
Panama. It led to a series of amendments to the Hay-Bunau-
Varilla Treaty and eventually to a major Panama Canal Treaty, the
Carter-Torrijos Treaties that became effective in 1979.

The first ship to go through the canal was the S.S. *Ancón*,
property of the Panama Railroad Company. It completed the trip
in 9 hours, 40 minutes. In 1939, the *Bremen*, a German ship of the
Hapag-Lloyd Lines, set a record as the largest ship ever to go
through the canal. However, this record was broken by the *Queen
Elizabeth II* in 1975. Toll payments for ships going through are
made according to tonnage. The *Queen Elizabeth II* holds the
dubious honor of paying the highest toll of any passenger ship:

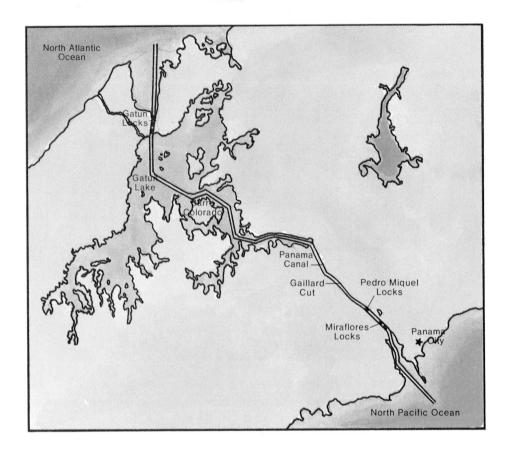

$42,077.88. The lowest toll was paid by a man who was given permission to swim the canal in 1928. The longest ship to transit was the *San Juan Prospector*, which is 973 feet (297 meters) long. The story of the canal can be seen in the murals painted on the walls of the Administrative Building of Balboa.

The approximate mileage saved between Japan and New York, if sailing by way of the canal, is 3,330 nautical miles (6,166 kilometers) and between Chile and Western Europe, 1,450 nautical miles (2,686 kilometers).

THE CANAL ZONE

The Canal Zone, the strip of land on either side of the waterway, is where North Americans connected in any way to the canal or to the defense of the territory have lived. It operated until the Carter-Torrijos Treaties as United States territory under U.S. civil and military laws.

During World War II, the Trans-Isthmian Highway was built. The Panamerican Highway comes from the north and goes through Panama, but it has not been continued from Panama into Colombia.

In 1950 the Panama Canal Company was incorporated and the Panamanian Railroad and all its commercial operations were turned over to the Canal Company. This company operated the waterway and supporting facilities while the Canal Zone administered all civic functions. The Panama Canal Commission replaced the Canal Company in 1979. The commission remains fully committed to serving world trade with high standards of excellence. The waterway should continue to be a viable, economic, and practical means of transportation well into the future, although some politicians believe that it is becoming obsolete, and there is talk of some day building another canal—one at sea level—through the Darién.

Also in 1979 the Canal Zone and its government were abolished as a result of the signing of the Carter-Torrijos Treaties. Under the treaty terms, the railroad was transferred to the government of Panama. This railroad makes several trips a day and takes an hour and a half to cross the isthmus.

The Panama Canal, whose motto is "The land divided, the world united," remains to this day one of the major accomplishments of engineering. It has been beneficial to many countries and, certainly, to Panama. It has been the cause of much friction between Panama and the United States. It is to be hoped that the implementation of the Carter-Torrijos Treaties will finally create a climate of good will between the two countries.

Chapter 7

PANAMA IN THE TWENTIETH CENTURY

THE CONSTITUTION OF 1904

On February 1, 1904, a constitution was adopted that contained a provision authorizing United States intervention in Panama if any disorder should break out. The constitution provided for a centralized authority to appoint and dismiss provincial governors. The constitutional convention of 1904 unanimously elected Manuel Amador Guerrero as president.

Subsequent elections were not quite that smooth and, in several instances, the United States's military forces had to intervene to help keep order. In 1925 a strange happening occurred. A U.S. citizen, Richard O. Marsh, led some of the Cuna Indians in San Blas in an uprising against the Panamanian government. They created the so-called Republic of Tule under a United States protectorate. The uprising was quickly squelched and the Republic of Tule dissolved.

Arnulfo Arias (left) was forced from office and succeeded by Ricardo de la Guardia (right) who also was forced from office.

A NEW CONSTITUTION

During the years that followed the establishment of the republic, there were many internal upheavals. In June 1940 Arnulfo Arias, a Harvard-educated physician, was elected president and changed the constitution to suit his purpose and also to increase his power. In October 1941 Arias was forcefully removed from office—the first of several times—and Ricardo de la Guardia, the minister of justice, succeeded him until he himself was exiled.

WORLD WAR II

Panama followed the United States into World War II after the Japanese attacked Pearl Harbor. During World War II, the United States requested sites for facilities such as landing fields, antiaircraft batteries, and warning stations. After the war the Panamanian National Assembly, influenced by the threat of violence on the part of the people, rejected the agreement previously reached about these sites.

PANAMANIAN PRESIDENTS AND POLITICS

In January 1951 de la Guardia returned from exile and there was a power struggle between him and President Arias, who was again president. The head of the police force, José A. Remón, emerged as a strong figure. Unrest and chaos were constant. After a run on the government-supported savings bank, de la Guardia was arrested. Remón overthrew Arias and succeeded him. In 1952 elections were held and Remón won a decisive victory. Remón undertook the transformation of the police into the National Guard or regular army. He was assassinated in 1955.

As in most Latin-American countries, students in Panama are often mixed in the political life of the country. In 1958 student riots led to a state of siege. A group of antigovernment students from the Instituto Nacional barricaded themselves inside the school and threw bombs made by the chemistry students out the window. The police replied with bullets and would not let anyone into the school. The students had no food for days. Eventually the police yielded and the incident was closed.

The 1960 presidential elections gave the victory to Roberto Chiari who, in turn, was followed in the next election by Marco Robles. By then, the Panamanian economy was faltering, unemployment was a serious problem, and the populace was restless.

A major event that took place in January 1964 was the "flag incident." According to a 1963 treaty, the Panamanian flag had to be flown next to the United States flag everywhere in the Canal Zone. However one evening, when a group of Panamanian students insisted on raising their flag in a school within the Canal Zone, some U.S. students and police beat them and tore up the

In 1964 students from the University of Panama demonstrate over ownership of the canal. The banner says "The canal is ours!"

Panamanian flag. Tempers flared in frustration over what had always been a thorn in the side of Panamanians: the apparent perpetuation of the U.S. exercise of rights in the Canal Zone. The Panamanians believed there should be sovereignty for their country. Terrible riots followed and both Panamanians and North Americans were killed. Panama broke off diplomatic relations temporarily with the United States.

In 1968 Arias won the elections again, but once more his victory was short-lived. He was removed from office and the military took over the control of the government, forming a military junta and dissolving the National Assembly.

Since 1972 Panama has had a new constitution (the nation's fourth), amended in 1978 and 1983. According to this constitution, Panama is a democratic republic. However, for more than two decades, it was ruled by a military dictatorship that began on October 11, 1968 when a coup destroyed the legal system. This coup was performed by the National Guard.

*The new Panama Canal Treaty was signed at the Organization of
American States in 1977. Torrijos is seated, third from right.*

General Omar Torrijos emerged as the leader. He was a
policeman, educated in the United States, who had worked his
way up the ranks. During Torrijos's period as head of the armed
forces, he made sure that a reliable friend was chosen to lead the
civil government junta and, eventually, be made president. This
was Demetrio Lakas.

Torrijos's main claim to fame, however, was his negotiations
with United States President Jimmy Carter that led to the 1977
signing of a new Panama Canal Treaty, the ratification of the
treaty in 1978, and the beginning of its implementation in 1979. It
was a process that had been going on for several years, but soon
after Carter was elected the process was accelerated, and the treaty
signed on September 7, 1977. The new basic treaty provided for
the gradual transfer of canal operations to Panamanians, the
phasing out of U.S. military bases, and the ultimate change of
hands and administration for the land and water used in the
management of the canal. By the same token, Panama was to
assume, by degrees, jurisdiction and responsibility over the
former Canal Zone.

An additional pact stating that the canal would stay open and neutral for all nations whether in peace or war also was signed. The treaty also stipulated that United States troops would be phased out by December 31, 1999. In addition, the United States had the right to intervene unilaterally with military force, if they believed that the lives of United States nationals were at risk, whether in the former Canal Zone or elsewhere in Panama. The transfer of the canal from United States hands to Panamanian hands was to be completed by the year 2000. The final signing ceremonies, after the ratification of the treaties by the United States Senate, were observed in Panama City on June 16, 1978.

General Torrijos strengthened the power of the armed forces during his administration by increasing the number of enlisted men, as well as weaponry. Torrijos died in a plane crash in 1981. General Manuel Antonio Noriega took Torrijos's place. Noriega has been accused of plotting Torrijos's death, although it has never been proven. Noriega was an informer on the CIA's payroll for many years.

Noriega continued Torrijos's process of building up the armed forces. The senior National Guard, which included five thousand police officers, became the Panama defense forces. This included a combination of police-military and paramilitary forces totaling approximately twenty-five thousand, creating a ratio of one soldier for every eighty citizens. The militarization of Panama was, in great part, the source of many problems the country experienced during the 1980s and into the 1990s.

The Panama defense forces, in their inception, were trained, armed, and financed by the United States government. However the involvement of top Panamanian officers in political murders, graft, and drug and weapons trafficking changed the United States's conception of the military relationship between the two countries. Noriega's power grew day by day through force. He is reported to have taken part in — or condoned — blackmail, torture, murder, imprisonment of political foes, and secret deals with Colombia's Medellín drug cartel, Cuba's Fidel Castro, Nicaragua's former president Manuel Ortega, and Libya's Muammar al-Qaddafi.

On May 6, 1984 presidential elections were held. The Electoral Tribunal, acting on Noriega's instructions, defrauded candidate Arias of a fair election. A year later, a heinous crime occurred that raised the population's consciousness and awareness of its rulers' immorality: Dr. Hugo Spadafora was decapitated after being tortured. He had been an active and vocal government opponent, publicly accusing General Noriega of repression, corruption, drug trafficking, and electoral fraud. This assassination caused a great uproar in the country.

In June 1987 Noriega deposed Colonel Roberto Díaz Herrera, army chief of staff, who had been Noriega's right-hand man. Furious at what had happened, Díaz Herrera decided to talk. He went to the media and declared that Noriega was responsible for Spadafora's murder, that Noriega was involved in drug and arms trafficking, and that there had been fraud in the last elections. This opened the eyes of anyone in Panama who was not already convinced of Noriega's guilt.

In July 1987 the civic crusade was born in Panama. Labor leaders, businessmen, professionals, students, and laborers were part of it. The aim of the crusade was to organize a political opposition to the military regime based on non-violent activism. It was ostensibly a reaction against the dictatorship's strong repression of political parties. Its struggle was characterized by peaceful demonstrations such as the one where everyone wore

*General Manuel Antonio Noriega (center, in military uniform and cap)
at a rally held in his honor in Panama City in 1989*

white as a peace symbol in contrast to the military's green
uniforms. Many Panamanians joined the crusade and there never
were signs of violence on their part, even though Noriega made
constant use of it.

When the United States clearly assessed Noriega's role as drug
trafficker, the state of Florida indicted him in February 1988 on
drug and racketeering charges. The indictment alleged that
Noriega was part of an international conspiracy with the Medellín
cartel to import cocaine into the United States.

On February 25, 1988 former President Eric del Valle tried to
fire Noriega as head of the Panamanian Defense Force, but instead
del Valle was ousted by a Congress that was under Noriega's
thumb. An ally of Noriega's, Solís Palma, was appointed
president—another puppet president. Shortly thereafter, the
government closed all the banks after massive withdrawals. This
caused great complications and deprivation for Panama's
population.

Colonel Leonidas Macías led a military coup, but it was squelched by Noriega's henchmen. There was an anti-Noriega march, for the people of Panama were becoming more and more desperate and hostile to Noriega. Some journalists and opposition leaders were brutally beaten.

In April 1988 the United States announced the application of economic sanctions and $56 million in Panamanian funds that were deposited in the United States were frozen.

So-called free presidential elections took place in Panama in May 1989 and the opposition candidate, labor lawyer Guillermo Endara, won easily with 70 percent of the vote. However, the Electoral Tribunal, acting on Noriega's orders, nullified the elections. The international observers who had come for the election process charged the government with fraud. Noriega retaliated by annulling the elections under the pretext of "foreign interference" on the part of the election observers. Three days after the election, the pro-Noriega civilian militia, called "Dignity Battalions," attacked the opposition candidates physically with lead pipes and wooden sticks as they were marching to protest the annulment of the election.

Immediately, President George Bush of the United States sent two thousand troops to reinforce the U.S. forces already stationed there. In September 1989 the Organization of American States (OAS) tried to reach a peaceful solution to the Panamanian question, but failed.

A coup that had been prepared by the oppositon for months was stifled in October 1989. Several rebel junior officers and troops tried to oust Noriega but failed. Noriega crushed the revolt and executed those involved. The world criticized President Bush for standing on the sidelines and doing nothing.

United States soldiers arriving in Panama in 1989

On December 15, 1989 the beginning of the end of the Noriega regime came with the declaration of a "state of war with the United States" from the Panamanian Congress and the nomination of General Noriega as "head of the government" and "chief executive officer." The next day some Panamanian officers killed a U.S. lieutenant without any provocation, except that he and three others with him had gotten lost.

Following the stipulations of the De Concini amendment of the 1977 Panama-United States Panama Canal Treaty, President Bush ordered a massive invasion of U.S. troops beginning the night and early morning of December 20, 1989. The White House stated that the mission was to protect U.S. lives, to seize Noriega, to restore democracy, and to preserve the integrity of the canal. It was called "Operation Just Cause."

Once the U.S. troops marched into Panama City, the armed resistance of Noriega's men was quickly reduced. It was mainly the "Dignity Battalions," made up, in great part, of common

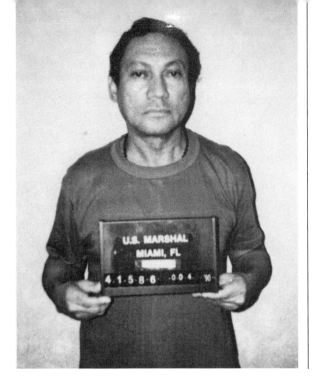

A mug shot of Noriega taken in Miami, Florida

criminals, who fought. Noriega himself eluded the manhunt. The United States government set a price on Noriega's capture: a reward of one million dollars. After three days of localized skirmishes and looting in the capital city of Panama, peace ensued. All the army barracks in the provinces surrendered by handing their keys to the local bishops.

On December 24, 1989 after hiding for a week, Noriega sought refuge at the *Nunciatura*, the Vatican Embassy in Panama City. The Bush administration demanded that the Papal Nuncio turn Noriega over to United States government officials to face charges in Florida for drug trafficking and money laundering.

On January 3, 1990 Noriega voluntarily left the Vatican Embassy and turned himself in to United States officials. Noriega was flown to Miami and arraigned. He had been indicted for drug trafficking by the United States in 1988 and offered a plea bargain, which he refused. Imprisoned at Miami's Metropolitan Center, he faced a long trial. On July 10, 1992, he was convicted on 8 of 10 drug and racketeering charges and sentenced to 40 years in prison.

Chapter 8

PANAMA'S ECONOMY

Panama is a small country with great financial activity. It occupies a place in world trade, world banking, and world financial services far beyond its size. If compared with other small countries, it is a rapidly developing country.

In Panama, a goodly proportion of the labor force is engaged in agricultural pursuits. Many work in service occupations such as banking, trade, tourism, transportation, communication, and public administration. Another part of the population works in manufacturing and, of course, the canal.

AGRICULTURE AND LIVESTOCK FARMING

Much of the population of Panama is involved in agriculture. Large modern commercial enterprises use state-of-the-art agricultural methods. Small farmers are still tilling the land in an old-fashioned way. Unfortunately there are Indians who still use the slash-and-burn type of agriculture. And there are other Indians who live within the framework of a nomadic and subsistence type of agriculture.

Cattle graze in the countryside surrounding Portobelo.

Most of the farming is done on a small scale. The main crops cultivated in Panama are corn, rice, beans, coffee, cocoa, sugarcane, coconuts, tobacco, citrus fruits, potatoes, yucca, tomatoes, and especially bananas, one of Panama's foremost sources of income. A large tract of land owned by an American company, the Chiriquí Land Company (formerly United Fruit Company), is devoted to growing enormous quantities of bananas that are sent in refrigerated ships all over the world with the label Chiquita on them. A plant called abaca provides the strongest natural fiber in the world.

The livestock industry, mainly cattle, has grown considerably in Panama. Besides cattle, the industry includes raising pigs and chickens.

FISHING

The fishing industry, particularly shrimp, is very important, as is the production of fish meal. Both are exported. Also abundant are tortoise shells, sponges, and pearls.

Fishermen weighing their catch (left) and exotic shells for sale in an island market

FORESTRY

Timber is another source of wealth in Panama where there are many species of trees that produce precious woods. Unfortunately, the excesses in this area, as well as those caused by cattle ranchers who destroy woods in order to have more grazing land for their cattle, is causing severe deforestation in Panama. This is a world problem that is far from being solved.

MINING AND INDUSTRY

Mining in Panama is limited to gold, manganese, and copper. There are salt deposits that constitute a considerable source of revenue. The chief industries in the country are sheet metal, cement and cement blocks, bathroom fixtures, shrimp and sardine processing and packaging, sugar refineries, oil refineries and oil derivatives, vegetable oils, clothing, and beer.

BANKING AND THE ECONOMY

Panama has had an extremely active banking system, which brought into the country more than 135 banks from all over the world. Panamanian banks follow former Swiss banking laws, and there are secret numbered accounts. These banks facilitate loans for all countries of the world. One of the chief assets for world banking is the fact that Panama's currency is worth the same as the United States dollar. It has been said that "when the United States sneezes, Panama catches a cold." The Panamanian currency is called a balboa, which does not exist in paper form, only in coins. It is minted in the United States. There are many financial companies headquartered in Panama that offer all types of services, as well as many insurance companies.

In 1988—a time of political unrest in Panama—the United States government put economic sanctions on the Noriega government, and this partially paralyzed the banking system. Assets were frozen but, little by little, monetary transactions have gone back to normalcy. However, many foreign banks have left Panama because the unstable political situation did not create a favorable environment in which to conduct banking.

Panama is a country that facilitates the forming of companies or corporations that do not pay taxes, so that people from many countries start their businesses with a Panamanian charter without even having to set foot in that country. Panama does not treat foreigners any differently than Panamanian nationals.

The same is true of Panama's merchant marine. Panama's ship registry exceeds fifty million gross tons, placing that country in second place in the world, trailing only Liberia. These ships are for the most part foreign-owned but they sail under the

Luxurious resorts and cruise ships attract tourists to Panama.

Panamanian flag because they pay lower tolls when passing through the canal. For lending its registry and flag to these ships, Panama collects substantial fees.

TOURISM AND CONVENTIONS

Panama offers a balmy climate, good beaches, lovely mountains, and a unique sight such as the canal. The archaeological, anthropological, and sociological interests offered by the presence of its Indians, wonderful music, food and drink, gambling, exceptional shopping bargains, and sports galore make the country a vacationer's dream.

For that reason, the tourism industry is a main source of income for Panama. The majority of tourists come from Central and South America, followed by United States citizens (mainly from southern states), and then Europeans and Asians. Cruise ships from North America often stop near the San Blas Islands or go through the canal.

If Panama has always been considered the "Heart of the Universe" and "Crossroads of the World" for the purpose of trade, it is now also being used as an international meeting place and is, therefore, an important convention center. The ATLAPA convention center near Panama City constantly hosts conventioneers from all over the world. Visitors to Panama will find that Panamanians are avid lottery players.

TRANSPORTATION

Panama is a major aviation as well as navigation center. Twenty international airlines plus COPA, a local airline, fly to and from Panama's Tocumen (formerly Omar Torrijos) International Airport. There are 126 smaller airports in the country.

Because of the number of ships that dock at Cristóbal and Balboa, as well as those that go through the canal, Panama constitutes one of the largest navigation centers of the world.

Panama's main highway is part of the Panamerican Highway that starts in Alaska, goes through Mexico and Central America and Panama. In Panama the highway starts at the Costa Rican border. As it reaches Panama City, it is linked by the famous Bridge of the Americas, built in 1958 to take the place of a ferry boat, the Thatcher ferry. The road goes as far as Chepo. The remainder of the road, from Chepo to the San Pablo Isthmus in Colombia, is yet to be completed. This 215-mile (346-kilometer) uncompleted section of the Panamerican Highway that must go through largely uninhabited jungle and marsh territory is known as the Darién Gap. There are many explanations as to why it has not been built yet and they do not all have to do with the ruggedness of the terrain. Some think that the Panamanian

The Panamerican Highway passes through the highlands of Panama.

government does not want to facilitate any movement of cattle from across the Colombian border because there has been anthrax and hoof-and-mouth disease in Colombia. The Trans-Isthmian Highway linking the two oceans was completed in 1942 and inaugurated in 1943 when driving was changed from the left-hand side of the road to the right-hand side.

The Panamanian railroad goes from the cities of Panama to Colón. It is the oldest transcontinental railway on the American continent. It was built in 1849 and after being operated for years by the United States Canal Company, it was returned to Panama

Passengers boarding the Panamanian railroad at Colón

after the Carter-Torrijos Treaty was signed. It is used both for passengers and freight.

A fact of great importance to the oil industry of the world was the building, in 1982, of a pipeline in Panama that carries underground the "black gold" that is shipped from Alaska to other parts of the world. It was built because many supertankers go through the canal. It has been a great contribution to Panama's economy and is the second largest income-producing company after the canal.

COLÓN FREE ZONE

The *Zona Libre de Colón,* "Colón Free Zone," is a very heavily guarded area that has been a boon to Panama's economy since it was created in 1948 by President Enrique Jiménez. The area takes up about one-fourth of the city of Colón. It is the most active and biggest trading zone on the American continent and a world center of commerce. Strategically located close to the port of Cristóbal on the Atlantic, it enjoys wide-ranging commercial success and it makes optimum use of Panama's geographical position. In the free zone, there are more than seven hundred companies that operate but no one lives there. The free zone's operations consist of receiving goods from abroad that can be processed, assembled, repackaged, warehoused, or exhibited, and then sent on to other countries without having to pay Panamanian taxes or duties. It is, in a way, the central clearinghouse of the world, where chemical products, machinery, transportation equipment, and manufactured articles, to name but a few, are brought in from the United States, Japan, England, and Germany, only to be sent to Central or South America, Panama itself, and other countries of the world. Tourists who buy in the free zone have their goods delivered to them when exiting the country. The free zone provides employment to thousands of Panamanians and deals in merchandise worth more than eight billion dollars annually.

PANAMA'S FUTURE

Panama's resources as well as its international commercial and financial activities have developed extraordinarily since the beginning of the twentieth century. The country offers services to its own inhabitants, as well as to the rest of the world but the canal still remains an enormous source of employment and the most important single factor in the nation's economy.

It is much to be desired that a land rich in natural resources and a people rich in resourcefulness, as well as a peace-loving one, will be able to live in prosperity and calm in the years to come, free from the unrest and turmoil brought upon by a sometimes chaotic political situation.

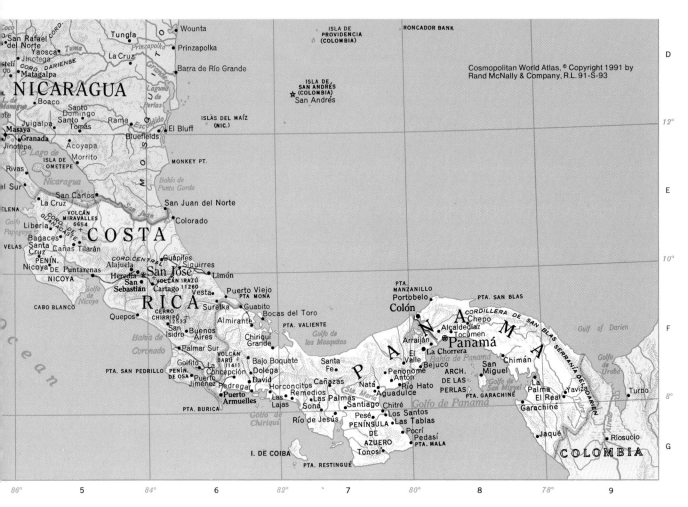

MAP KEY

MINI-FACTS AT A GLANCE

GENERAL INFORMATION

Official Name: Republic of Panama

Capital: Panama City

Official Language: Spanish

Government: Panama is governed by the constitution of 1972 and it is designated as a republic with a presidential form of government. In 1983 the constitution was revised, reducing the presidential term from six to five years and abolishing the National Assembly of Community Representatives in favor of a more compact Legislative Assembly. It has 72 members elected for five-year terms.

Panama is divided into nine provinces: Bocas del Toro, Chiriquí, Coclé, Colón, Darién, Herrera, Los Santos, Panamá, and Veraguas, and the special Indian territory of Territory Commarce de San Blas. Each province is under a governor and a deputy governor appointed by the president.

Flag: The flag is made up of four rectangles: lower left, blue; upper right, red; upper left, white with blue star in center; and lower right, white with red star in center.

National Anthem: *"Himno Nacional de la Republica de Panamá,"* also called *"Hímno Istmeño"* ("National Hymn of the Republic of Panama")

Religion: Roman Catholicism. The country's religous minorities include Protestants, Jews, Buddhists, Hindus, and Muslims.

Money: The basic unit of currency is the balboa. The United States dollar is also used. In 1994 one balboa was worth one U.S. dollar.

Weights and Measures: Panama uses the metric system.

Population: 1990 census—2,329,329; estimated 1994—2,607,000 (53 percent urban; 47 percent rural)

Principal Cities:
Panama City	625,150
San Miguelito	243,025*
Colón	137,825

(Population based on 1992 estimates; *1990 census.)

119

GEOGRAPHY

Highest Point: Volcán Barú, 11,401 ft. (3,475 m)

Lowest Point: Sea level along the coasts

Mountains: Two mountain ranges form a continental backbone, the Cordillera Central from the Costa Rica border almost to Panama City and the lower Cordillera de San Blas from east of Colón to the Colombian border. (The Panama Canal runs through the gap between them.)

Rivers: Approximately 500 rivers have their sources in the highlands—the Tuira, Bayano, Sixaola, Changuinola, Chiriquí Viejo, and Santa María. About one-third flow into the Atlantic and two-thirds flow into the Pacific. Only the Tuira is navigable for long distances. The Chagres River is one of the longest and most vital and is a major source of hydroelectric power, as is the Chepo.

Climate: Tropical weather systems in the Caribbean carry warm, humid air over the isthmus throughout the year. The northern slopes of the two mountain systems receive an average of 128 in. (325 cm) of rainfall a year, whereas the southern slopes receive only about half that much (about 68 in.—173 cm). There are often violent thunderstorms during the summer. Temperatures remain quite constant—from 77° to 80° F. (25° to 26.6° C) at Panama City.

Greatest Distances: East to west: 410 mi. mi. (660 km)
North to south: 130 mi. (209 km)

Area: 29,762 sq. mi. (77,082 km²)

NATURE

Trees: More than half of the country is covered with a tropical rain forest. There are many trees in Panama, including mangrove trees, cativo, mahogany, kapok, tagua, cashew, and orey. The drier Pacific Coast has some deciduous trees, while on the wet Caribbean side, the trees are evergreen. There are over 2,000 flowering plants, including the national orchid, called the Holy Ghost.

Animals: On Barro Colorado Island there is a treasure trove of animals, reptiles, and insects: crocodiles, giant anteaters, bush dogs, ocelots, jaguars, monkeys, tapirs, bats, and sloths; frogs; lizards and snakes; grasshoppers, bedbugs, termites, and cockroaches.

Fish: Panama's rich fishing grounds along the Pacific and Atlantic coasts abound in over 50 varieties of commercially valuable fish including: shrimp, mackerel, anchovy, tuna, grouper, barracuda, pompano, sailfish, and sea bass.

EVERYDAY LIFE

Food: Rice is the most important food and most Panamanian dishes use rice as their major ingredient. Beef and pork are eaten in almost all localities and by all income groups, but chicken and eggs are consumed mostly by urbanites. Fish and seafood are abundant and are prepared in many varied and delicious ways. Fruit and vegetables are bountiful—and flavorful. The national beverage is beer, but palm wine, rum, and *chicha* (fermented from corn) are also popular.

Housing: Rural Panamanians live in small one or two-room cottages with thatch roofs and walls made of sugarcane stalks or branches held together with clay or mud. Poor urban people live in shacks or run-down tenements. Well-to-do urban residents live in large houses built in Spanish-colonial or modern architectural style.

Holidays:

January 1, New Year's Day
January 9, Martyrs' Day
March 1, Constitution Day
May 1, Labor Day
October 11, Revolution Day
October 12, Columbus Day
November 28, Independence Day
December 8, Mothers' Day
December 25, Christmas Day

Culture: Panamanian culture has a Hispanic base with strong African, Indian, and non-Hispanic Western influences. Folk music and dance are especially popular. In the *tamborita*, the national dance, couples are accompanied by drums playing intricate, contrapuntal rhythms.

Many of the best examples of colonial architecture have not been carefully maintained, and after World War II an international style was developed that was suitable for tropical conditions. The campus of the University of Panama is an example.

The Museum of the Panamanian Man was established in 1976 to exhibit archaeology and ethnography.

Sports and Recreation: Baseball is the most popular sport, but soccer is loved as well. Fishing, sailing, and scuba diving draw many participants. Horses are ridden by many, young and old alike, and horse racing is a favorite spectator sport. Cockfights and boxing also draw large and enthusiastic audiences.

Communication: The constitution guarantees freedom of speech, press, and other forms of communication. The national government owns and operates the telegraph system and the telephone system.

Transportation: There are two railroads, one owned by the Panamanian government, the other by the Chiriquí Land Company, a subsidiary of United Brands. The two major ports are Cristóbal and Balboa. There are 500 mi. (805 km) of navigable inland waterways of which the Panama Canal accounts for 51 mi. (82 km). The main highways are the Trans-Isthmian Highway that links Colón and Panama City and the National, or Central Highway, which is the Panamanian section of the Panamerican Highway. There are four domestic airlines — Panama Air International, Companía Panameña de Aviación (COPA), Aerolíniaeas Pacífico Atlántico, SA (Aeroperlas), and Dirección de Aeronaútica Civil.

Education: Education is free, universal, and compulsory for children between the ages of 7 and 15. There are six years of primary school, three years of lower secondary school, and three years of upper secondary school. Primary school teachers are trained in normal schools and secondary school teachers are trained at the University of Panama. Higher education is provided at the University of Panama and the University of Santa María la Antigua.

Health and Welfare: The principal health problems are tuberculosis, pneumonia, malaria, leprosy, cancer, and mental illness. Most of the population has access to modern medical care. Health services are directed by the Ministry of Health, advised by the National Commission for Health Planning. Health standards are among the highest in Latin America.

ECONOMY AND INDUSTRY

Principal Products:
Agriculture: Bananas, sugarcane, beans, corn, rice, coffee
Manufacturing: Food and drink processing, metal working, petroleum products, chemicals, paper and paper products, printing, mining, refined sugar, clothing, furniture

IMPORTANT DATES

1513—Vasco Núñez de Balboa reaches Pacific by crossing Panama

First half of the 17th Century—Colonial Panama reaches prosperity

18th Century—Panama declines as South American ports develop trade with Spain

1821—Panama wins independence from Spain; Panama joins Colombia, Venezuela, and Ecuador in voluntary incorporation

1826—Congress of Panama; U.S. makes known its interest in having canal built

1830—Union with Colombia, Venezuela, and Ecuador breaks up, but Panama remains part of Colombia

1840s—U.S. discovery of gold in California and drive toward Pacific revives interest in a short crossing between the Atlantic and Pacific oceans

1840s—U.S. discovery of gold in California and drive toward Pacific revives interest in a short crossing between the Atlantic and Pacific oceans

1855—Panama Railroad opens; U.S. presence in Panama begins

1879—Ferdinand de Lesseps, builder of the Suez Canal, forms a company to construct similar waterway in Panama

1880—Work on the canal begins

1889—The French company working on the canal collapses

1901—U.S. commits itself to the canal

1903—Panamanian leaders declare independence from Colombia; U.S. signs Hay-Herrán Treaty agreeing to provide military protection in exchange for exclusive right to build a canal

1904—Panama adopts constitution authorizing U.S. to intervene in Panama to maintain peace and protect property

1904—Manuel Amador Guerrero becomes president, disbands army, adopts dollar as currency; Canal Zone transferred to U.S. jurisdiction

1914—Panama Canal opens

1924—Victoria-Velez Treaty between Panama and Colombia is signed

1925—Cuna Indians fight war against Panama

1926—Congress of Panama

1931—Traditional elites lose their monopoly on power; the Arias brothers, Harmodio and Arnulfo, assume political control

1940—Arnulfo Arias is elected president; he challenges U.S. by refusing to cooperate in defense preparations prior to U.S. entry into World War II

1941—Arias-Calderón Treaty; Arias is removed from office; the U.S. receives defense sites that are later returned

1946—Liberal constitution embodies reforms

1940s and 1950s—Panama tries to diversify its dependence on canal

1950—Panama Canal Company is incorporated

1955—New Treaty raises canal annuity paid to Panama

1958-59—Anti-U.S. riots

1960-64—Elites headed by President Robert Chiari adopt limited social and economic reforms

1964—Serious anti-U.S. riots erupt

1964-68—Administration of Marcos Robles presses for domestic reforms and pursues treaty negotiations with U.S.

1969—General Omar Torrijos becomes president; governs as a dictator

1969—General Omar Torrijos becomes president; governs as a dictator

1979—Carter-Torrijos Treaties signed with U.S.; Canal Zone and its government abolished; neutrality of canal guaranteed after 1999

1981—Torrijos killed in a plane crash; General Manuel Antonio Noriega comes to power

1987—Civic crusade in opposition to Noriega is born

1988—Noriega is indicted in the United States "in absentia" for drug trafficking and racketeering

1989—U.S. troops invade Panama

1990—Noriega is brought to the United States and faces trial; Guillermo Endara becomes president

1992—Noriega is convicted of drug and racketeering charges and sentenced to 40 years in jail

1993—Voters defeat proposed constitutional reforms, which included prohibition of the army

1994—An American-educated banker and government minister, Ernesto Perez Balladares of the Revolutionary Democratic Party (PRD) is elected president; he promises social reforms and a market orientated economy geared to job creation in rural areas; the Endara government is accused of corruption; Panama grants asylum to deposed Haitian junta leaders and their families at United States's request

1995—United States upgrades Panama's position for economic benefits as country has fully cooperated with United States in instituting money-laundering controls; repair work on a set of locks on Panama Canal causes considerable delays in ship traffic

IMPORTANT PEOPLE

Manuel Amador Guerrero (1833-1909), elected president, 1904

Pedro de Anglería (1455-1526), chronicler of the colonial period

Arnulfo Arias (1897-1988), president 1940-41, 1949-51, 1968

Harmodio Arias (1886-1962), president 1932-36

Pedro Arias Dávila (?1440-1531), known as Pedrarias, governor of Golden Castille (Panama)

Manuel J. de Ayala (1726-1805), early writer and lawmaker

Vasco Núñez de Balboa (1475-1519), explorer; first European to see and explore the Pacific Ocean

Rodrigo de Bastidas (1460-1526), Spanish explorer, discoverer of Panama in 1501

Rodolfo Chiari (1869-1937), president 1924-31

Juan de la Cosa (?1460-1510), pilot and navigator with Rodrigo de Bastidas

Hernando de la Cruz (1591-1646), Jesuit priest, early eighteenth-century poet

Ricardo de la Guardia (1899-1969), minister of justice, president 1941

Jerónimo de la Ossa, poet who wrote lyrics of the national anthem

Roberto Díaz Herrera, army chief of staff, deposed by Noriega in 1987

Martín Fernández de Enciso (?1470-1528) founded first town in Panama, Tierra Firme, in 1510

David DeBose Gaillard (1859-1913), chief engineer of Panama Canal

Dr. William Gorgas (1854-1920), U.S. doctor who freed area of disease before work on the canal began

Ferdinand de Lesseps (1805-94), first builder of the Panama Canal

Diego de Nicuesa (?-1511), conquistador sent by Spanish crown to govern Golden Castille (present-day Panama)

General Manuel Antonio Noriega (1934-   ), in 1981 became dictator at Torrijos' death; deposed in 1989

María Olimpia de Obaldía, writer and essayist

Alfonso de Ojeda (1465-1515), conquistador sent by Spanish crown to govern area that is present-day Colombia

Basilio de Oviedo (1478-1557), chronicler of the colonial period

José A. Remón (1908-55), head of police force; assassinated 1955

Omar Torrijos (1929-81), president 1972-81; signed treaties with U.S. President Jimmy Carter in 1977 turning over canal to Panama in 1999

W.B. Van Ingen (1858-?), muralist who depicted construction of the canal

Lucien Napoléon Bonaparte Wyse (1845-1909), signed treaty with Colombia in 1878 for study of canal across the isthmus

INDEX

Page numbers that appear in boldface type indicate illustrations

About the Author

Ana María Brull Vázquez was born in Cuba. Because her father was a Cuban diplomat, she lived with her family in many other countries. A graduate of the University of Ottawa in Canada, Mrs. Vázquez received her master's degree in history from the University of Fribourg in Switzerland. Upon her return to Cuba, she directed the manuscript department of the Lobo Napoleonic Museum in Havana, developed radio programs for the Ministry of Education, and wrote numerous articles for Havana magazines. Forced into exile because of the Communist takeover, Mrs. Vázquez worked as associate editor of *The Guidepost*, an American magazine published in Madrid, Spain.

A resident of Chicago for thirty-one years, Mrs. Vázquez has been a free-lance writer for radio and televison, an editor and translator, a college Spanish teacher, and a volunteer worker for a variety of cultural programs. She has worked in advertising and as a consultant on international matters. She has raised her three children, Alejandro, Isabel, and Jaime, in a totally bilingual and bicultural environment.

Mrs. Vázquez was awarded the Cross of Queen Isabella of Spain by King Juan Carlos I in recognition of her accomplishments.